THE POINT OF CHRISTOLOGY

To

JOHN DESCHNER

beloved companion on the way

Contents

Preface

Except for changes required to transform them into a book, the following chapters were delivered during Trinity Term 1980–81 as the Sarum Lectures at the University of Oxford. Earlier series of lectures on the same topic were given in 1975 as the Lewis French Stearns Lectures at Bangor Theological Seminary and in 1979 as the Frances Youngker Vosburgh Lectures at Drew University. Also, the originals of what are now Chapters 5 through 8, under the title "For Freedom Christ Has Set Us Free," constituted the 1981 Fondren Lectures at Southern Methodist University.

To all the persons to whom I owe the invitations to do these lectures I am deeply grateful. The opportunities they provided to fill out the christological outline I projected some two decades ago in *Christ without Myth* allowed me to discharge an obligation that I have long felt to myself as well as to others. I am also grateful to the many other persons who participated in the actual delivery of the lectures. The comments and questions I received from them following the earlier series played an important role in working out the form and the content of the final argument. I also think with particular gratitude of the two persons who were chiefly responsible for the rich experience that was my wife's and mine during the four weeks we spent in Oxford: Professor Basil Mitchell, who, as Chairman of the Sarum Electors, was our unfailingly cordial host; and Professor Maurice Wiles, who regularly interrupted a precious term of leave to attend my lectures and to give me the benefit of his critical reactions to them.

In preparing the lectures I tried to keep in mind that, according to the statute governing the post of the Sarum Lecturer, I was supposed to deliver eight "theological lectures in support of the Christian faith." In this connection I was mindful, above all, of two kinds of persons, whom I cannot but still think of in now issuing the lectures as a book.

On the one hand, there are those who regard themselves as non-Christians and who, whenever they hear of the Christian faith, think first of all of the claims that Christians have historically made concerning Jesus himself. Because they are quite unable to come to terms with these claims, they never reach the point of being confronted by the offer of radical faith that is decisively re-presented to them through Jesus. On the other hand, there are those who would like to think of themselves as Christians and who either accept or at least are powerfully attracted by the offer of faith that is re-presented to them through Jesus, only to continually doubt whether they can really call themselves Christians after all. For even though they are willing to trust their lives to the mysterious ultimate reality encompassing them, and to love both themselves and their neighbors in their returning love for this same ultimate reality, they are not able to accept the claims that Christians have historically made about Jesus himself.

Whether what is said in the following pages is likely to speak to the needs of these kinds of persons I will not presume to judge. But I am quite clear that it is to just such persons, both within and without the churches, that any argument today in support of the Christian faith most espe-

cially needs to be addressed; and I shall feel more than re-
warded for writing this book if any of my readers who is
sensible of such needs in his or her person finds anything in
what I have tried to say that is at all helpful in meeting them.

I should perhaps also emphasize here, to avoid any possible
misunderstanding, that this book neither is nor is intended to
be anything like the usual treatise on christology. Far from
being yet another attempt to formulate the doctrines of the
person and the work, the states and the offices, of Jesus
Christ, it is the very different kind of undertaking indicated
by its title: a critical inquiry into the *point* of all such doctrinal formulations. There can hardly be an urgent need for any
more christologies, whether revisionary or traditional, that
neglect to preface their formulations of doctrine with this
kind of critical inquiry. On the other hand, if the point of
christology is the existential point I here argue it is, one can
hardly fail to ask whether the usual treatise on the doctrine
of Christ can be anything like the preferred way in which to
try to make it.

This is the issue Dennis Nineham raises when he allows
that, to his mind, "the question *how* our relationship to God
came to be the way it is, *how* through Jesus of Nazareth God
produced this relationship with himself in the church, is a
question which scarcely deserves the high priority and the
enormous amount of attention that it seems to be receiving
in a great deal of contemporary theology. . . . our priority as
Christians, and as Christian theologians in contemporary
Western culture, should be the understanding of our relationship with God in a way which makes sense in our world.
It should be the attempt to practice our relationship with
God in a way that is compatible with the rest of our approach
to life" (McDonald [ed.]: 65 f.). If justification must be given
for the kind of christological reflection I have felt constrained
to pursue, I am content to appeal to the same theocentrism

and stress on *praxis* to which Nineham here gives forcible expression.

Of the other persons to whom I am indebted in completing this book, the students in my seminar in christology at Southern Methodist University in the fall semester 1980–81 deserve special mention. They were not only patient of the first drafts of lectures that I tried out on them, but by their own engagement in critically inquiring into the point of christology they helped to create the context in which my questions and answers took final shape. To one of them, Pamela Dickey Young, I am further indebted for suggesting the title of Chapter 7. Together with some of her sisters in Perkins School of Theology, she has for some time persistently, if always respectfully, tried to make me more sensitive to the unconscious sexism of some of my first attempts at theological formulation—in this instance, my choice as a title of the familiar New Testament phrase, "the God and Father of Our Lord Jesus Christ." Finally, I want to thank Betty Manning and Mary Ann Marshall, who once again capably did all of the typing—both of the lectures and of the book.

S.M.O.

Dallas, Texas
June 1981

It is not enough nor is it Christian, to preach the works, life, and words of Christ as historical facts, as if the knowledge of these would suffice for the conduct of life, although this is the fashion of those who must today be regarded as our best preachers. Far less is it enough or Christian to say nothing at all about Christ and to teach instead the laws of men and the decrees of the fathers. . . . Rather ought Christ to be preached to the end that faith in him may be established, that he may not only be Christ, but be Christ for you and me, and that what his name denotes may be effectual in us. Such faith is produced and preserved in us by preaching why Christ came, what he brought and bestowed, what benefit it is to us to accept him. This is done when that Christian freedom that he bestows is rightly taught, and we are told how we Christians are all kings and priests and therefore lords of all, and may firmly believe that whatever we have done is pleasing and acceptable in the sight of God. . . .

—MARTIN LUTHER, *Tractatus de libertate christiana*

1. The Problem of a Revisionary Christology

"But who do you say that I am?" So, according to the familiar account in Matthew's gospel, did Jesus inquire of his disciples, thereby evoking Peter's response, "You are the Christ, the Son of the living God" (16:15 f.). Significantly, the historical theologian Bernhard Lohse has found in the event represented by this account the starting point of the history of dogma, Peter's response being, as he says, "the first dogma in the sense of a confession" (Lohse: 16). The force of Lohse's finding obviously depends on the broad sense in which he uses the word "dogma" to mean simply confession of faith in Jesus as the Christ. But whether or not "dogma" is usefully construed so broadly, the word "christology" clearly has been and quite appropriately can be used in just such a broad sense. In fact, if we can say that in its obvious literal meaning "christology" means *logos* about *christos,* or thought and speech about Christ, we can say that the first and most fundamental sense of the word is sufficiently broad to cover any and all thought and speech about Jesus who is said to be Christ, as well as any number of other things such as the Prophet, the Servant of God, the Lord, the Son of Man, the Son of God, and even God. In this first, very broad sense even the relatively more spontaneous, less deliberate response to Jesus' question that Peter is represented as making is without doubt christology.

Of course, this first sense of the word is not its only sense, for it has also come to be used more strictly. Insofar as the relatively more spontaneous, less deliberate thought and

speech about Jesus, which are christology in the primary
sense, are themselves subjected to more or less critical reflection, one can speak of the emergence of christology in another, secondary sense. In this sense the word "christology"
covers not all thought and speech about Jesus, but only the
relatively less spontaneous, more deliberate thought and
speech that are necessarily involved in such critical reflection. "Christology" in this secondary sense, then, refers to
either the process or the product of critically reflecting on
the witness to Jesus as the Christ which is christology in the
primary sense of the word.

Clearly, in any account, the distinction between the one
christology and the other—let us say, the christology of witness and the christology of reflection—is by no means absolute. Even the most spontaneous witness to Jesus as the
Christ consists in thought and speech, and thus necessarily
involves some degree of reflection, however slight. On the
other hand, the thought and speech produced by even the
most deliberate critical reflection on such witness are themselves as product simply one more part of the witness on
which the ongoing process of christological reflection henceforth has to reflect. But if the distinction between the two
christologies is clearly relative rather than absolute, it is
nevertheless a real distinction and, in any theological account, important. This is emphatically so in the account that
informs the present discussion. Unlike most theologians past
and present, I feel bound to insist that the process of reflection on the witness of faith that is properly distinguished as
theology is fully critical only insofar as it is constituted not by
one question but by two: by asking not only about the *meaning* of the witness of faith but also about its *truth.*

What I mean by this can be further clarified by considering
briefly what is involved in critical reflection. In general, to
reflect critically means to take things that *appear* to be so and
then to ask more or less deliberately, methodically, and in a

reasoned way whether they really are so. Prominent among the ways in which things may appear to be so is that they are *said* to be so; and in this important special case, reflection not uncommonly takes the form of asking and answering two questions, the first in order to the second. One asks, first of all, what is really *meant* by what is said—what is meant and what is said never being simply the same—and then, secondly, whether what is meant really is the case, in the sense that things really are as they are meant to be by what is said about them. Because it is this second question about the truth of what is meant that is clearly *the* question of critical reflection—the first question about the meaning of what is said being asked and answered solely for the sake of it—I should suppose it mistaken to regard any process of reflection as fully critical that did not involve asking and answering the second question about truth.

But then for the same reason I can only regard what has usually been understood as theological reflection as something less than fully critical. In the conventional understanding, theology involves asking about the meaning of the witness of faith but not about its truth. As a matter of fact, as it has almost always been understood, theology is constituted not only as the product of critical reflection but even as the process thereof only by an affirmative answer to the question whether the witness of faith is really true. It follows that one cannot so much as ask the theological question unless one already believes the witness about whose meaning it inquires. Thus, in this usual understanding, the christology of witness and the christology of reflection, even though distinct, are still very close, insofar as the reflection the second involves is only partially critical, being concerned solely with the meaning of the first, never with its truth. In my understanding, by contrast, the distinction between the two christologies, even though relative, is still much sharper, insofar as the christology of reflection, being fully critical, asks about

the truth of the christology of witness as well as about its
meaning.

This is not the place to pursue the relevance of such an
understanding of theology to the frequently confused discussions of theological freedom and doctrinal discipline in the
life of the church. I have introduced it here mainly in order
to explain the principal task to which this book is offered as
a contribution. My intention in what follows is to further the
effort in our situation today toward a christology of reflection
that will be fully critical in that it will ask and answer the
question of the truth of the christology of witness as well as
the question of its meaning.

I can put this same point slightly differently in terms of the
two criteria of adequacy that, in my understanding of theology, any adequate christology of reflection must satisfy. On
the one hand, there is the criterion of *appropriateness,* which
requires of all the assertions of any such christology that they
so interpret what is meant by the christology of witness that
they are appropriate to its meaning as judged by its apostolic
norm. On the other hand, there is the criterion of *credibility,*
which requires of the same assertions that they all so formulate the claim to truth that the christology of witness ad-
vances that they are credible to human existence as judged
by common experience and reason. Put in these terms, my
main purpose is to help develop a christology of reflection
that, again, in our situation, will be credible as well as appropriate, because it answers for the truth of the christology of
witness as well as for its meaning.

All of this can be expressed more simply still by recalling
the title of the book. What I propose to do by means of the
christology of reflection that it is devoted to developing is,
quite simply, to make the point of the christology of witness
as theology today is given and called to make this point.

But to *make* the point of christology is one thing, to *talk
about* its point, as the title actually does, is something else.

Ordinarily we do not talk about the point of something unless, for one reason or another, either its meaning or its truth is somehow in doubt. As long as we grasp the meaning of what someone says or does, we do not talk about its point, at least in the sense in which we find ourselves doing so whenever what is said or done is, for whatever reason, simply meaningless to us, beyond our comprehension. Similarly, as long as we share the judgment that what someone says or implies is true, we do not talk about its point in the other sense in which we are quite likely to do so whenever, believing that what is said or implied is false, we find it, as we say, pointless, something that no one would go on saying or implying who knew the truth. It would certainly seem, then, that if one's talk about the point of christology is well advised, this must be because either the meaning or the truth of the christology of witness is more than ordinarily problematic.

Just this, however, clearly seems to me to be the case, and I cannot imagine that there is anything novel or unprecedented in my thinking so. For the better part of two centuries, theologians have widely regarded the normative forms of the christology of witness in scripture and tradition as sufficiently problematic that they have increasingly given themselves to the project of a revisionary christology that would replace or at least reformulate the traditional christology based on scripture and dogma. The main lines of this important development, which is of a piece with the emergence of revisionary theology generally, are sufficiently familiar that there is no need to rehearse them here. But it is to our purpose to be clear about where this development has now brought us; and the clearer we become about this, the clearer we will be why one can make the point of christology today only by also talking about it.

Speaking schematically, one may say that there are two main reasons why the traditional christology based on scripture and dogma has proved to be problematic. The first of

these reasons was definitively formulated by Rudolf Bultmann in accounting for the problem of contemporary theology by pointing to the emergence of the world-picture of
modern natural science and of a distinctively modern understanding of human existence. Taken together, Bultmann argued, our picture of the world as a lawfully regulated whole
and our understanding of our own self as a closed inner unity
are implicitly demythologizing, in that they imply both the
empirical falsity of all mythology and its existential irrele-
vance, insofar as it is taken to express a strictly empirical kind
of truth (Bultmann, 1951b). If this argument is to the point, as
I deem it to be, the christology of witness characteristic of the
New Testament is bound to be problematic for any of us
sharing a modern world-picture and self-understanding, because its conceptuality and symbolism are quite obviously
mythological and are evidently taken, in a great many cases
at any rate, to express the same kind of empirical truth as
science. Of course, to put the matter in this way is to run the
risk of anachronism, since all the relevant distinctions—between mythology and science, and between either of them
and self-understanding—are modern distinctions, which are
hardly made by the writers of the New Testament. But the
very fact that this is so is reason enough to explain why we
today are almost certain to have serious problems not only
with believing the christology of scripture but even with
understanding it. Insofar as its concepts and symbols are
mythological, and yet are not clearly and consistently recognized to be such, neither its meaning nor its truth can be
anything but a problem for us.

One may naturally question the extent to which, even in
the New Testament, the mythology taken over from Jewish
apocalypticism or from some form or other of Hellenistic
religiousness is, in effect, demythologized. And one is even
more justified in urging that the process whereby the mythological christology of scripture was reinterpreted in the dog-

mas of the trinity and of the divine-human person of Jesus Christ was to some extent a process of demythologizing. But even if one allows, as I certainly do, that there are at least verbal differences between the *myth* of incarnation and the *doctrine* of incarnation whereby the myth was interpreted metaphysically, one may point to yet a second main reason why the traditional christology incorporating this doctrine is deeply problematic for us today. I refer, namely, to the several difficulties that theologians from Friedrich Schleiermacher onward have repeatedly confirmed in the traditional doctrine of the incarnation. Of these difficulties three in particular may be singled out for comment.

The first is that the metaphysical conceptuality and symbolism in terms of which the doctrine of the incarnation has traditionally been formulated are now outmoded and in important respects inadequate. Paul Tillich, for example, claims that "the doctrine of the two natures in the Christ raises the right question but uses wrong conceptual tools." This is so, he explains, because what is properly meant by "the Christ-character of Jesus as the Christ" is not the "static essence" designated by "the inadequate concept 'divine nature,' " but rather the "dynamic relation" more adequately expressed by "the concepts 'eternal God-man-unity' or 'Eternal God-Manhood' " (Tillich, 1957: 142, 148). Other theologians such as Friedrich Gogarten, as alienated from Tillich's German idealism as from classical metaphysics, typically define the difficulty rather differently, by appealing against all metaphysics to some more "historical" conceptuality and symbolism as alone appropriate for christological formulation (Gogarten, 1966). Or, again, one thinks of theologians oriented to recent "process" metaphysics, whose critique of classical theism sharply challenges the fundamental axiom of the divine absoluteness and impassibility by which, as historians of doctrine have shown, the whole early development of traditional christology was profoundly determined (Pittenger, 1959:

146–175; Pelikan: 228–232). Clearly, there are various reasons
why theologians have problems with classical metaphysics,
and one could hardly agree with all of them. But the point
on which their criticisms converge is well taken: not only is
the metaphysics presupposed by the traditional doctrine of
the incarnation the thought-form of an age now past and thus
doubtfully credible, but it is also questionably appropriate for
making the point of the christology of witness that an adequate christology of reflection is supposed to make.

A second difficulty with the traditional doctrine of the incarnation is the one recently focused by several of the con-
tributors to *The Myth of God Incarnate.* The most provoca-
tive statement of it is by John Hick, who argues that
orthodoxy has never been able to give any real content to its
talk of Jesus as both God and man. "It remains a form of
words without assignable meaning. For to say, without explanation, that the historical Jesus of Nazareth was also God is
as devoid of meaning as to say that this circle drawn with a
pencil on paper is also a square. Such a locution has to be
given semantic content: and in the case of the language of
incarnation every content thus far suggested has had to be
repudiated. The Chalcedonian formula, in which the attempt rested, merely reiterated that Jesus was both God and
man, but made no attempt to interpret the formula" (Hick
[ed.]: 178). The effect of Hick's argument, as becomes still
clearer from his contribution to the continuing debate in
Incarnation and Myth, is to challenge the supposed distinction between the *doctrine* of the incarnation and the *myth*
or metaphor thereof as merely verbal. "What we receive
from our tradition," he claims, "is a broad imaginative motif
together with a history of attempts to spell it out. . . . But
when we turn from the general motif and its creative elabo-
ration in art, to theological science, we quickly observe that
there is nothing that can be called *the* Christian doctrine of
the incarnation. Indeed, the long history of the christological

debates is the story of the church's failure to achieve a clear
and agreed spelling out of the broad imaginative conception
that God was incarnate in Jesus the Jewish Messiah. . . . we
have the officially adopted metaphysical hypothesis of the
two natures, but no accepted account of what it means for an
individual to have two natures, one human and the other
divine. . . . the centuries-long attempt of Christian orthodoxy
to turn the metaphor into metaphysics was a cul-de-sac"
(Goulder [ed.]: 47–49). Hick's statement of the difficulty here
is perhaps extreme, and one notes that those of his collabora-
tors who comment on it are unwilling to go so far as to
compare the doctrine of the incarnation to a square circle (5,
54). Even so, I find as little reason as they do to dissent from
his essential point or to suppose that the logical difficulty he
so sharply focuses is anything but acute. At the least one may
say with Maurice Wiles that, "throughout the long history of
attempts to present a reasoned account of Christ as both fully
human and fully divine, the church has never succeeded in
offering a consistent or convincing picture" (Hick [ed.]: 4).

The third difficulty with the traditional doctrine of the
incarnation Wiles also brings out in the sentence immediately following: "Most commonly," he adds, "it has been the
humanity of Christ that has suffered; the picture presented
has been of a figure who cannot by our standards of judgment
(and what others can we apply?) be regarded as recognizably
human" (Hick [ed.]: 4). Wiles's point hardly requires elabora-
tion. It has been made so long and so often and is so widely
accepted as telling by the most diverse parties to christological discussion that it is not likely to be seriously questioned.
As a matter of fact, its full acceptance by many theologians
whose efforts are directed not to replacing the traditional
doctrine of the incarnation but to reformulating it accounts
for the development of the particular version of the traditional doctrine that increasingly seems to commend itself to
its contemporary defenders. I refer, of course, to what, since

its emergence in nineteenth-century Lutheran and Anglican theology, has generally been referred to as kenoticism. A principal motive of this form of incarnational doctrine has been to do justice to the full humanity of Jesus, as, by common consent, a traditional christology shaped by so-called neo-Chalcedonianism quite failed to do. But aside from the fact that kenoticist christologies could not do this at all except by in their own way revising traditional doctrine, there is serious question in the minds of some of us whether they have in any way overcome the second difficulty of such doctrine—the difficulty, namely, of developing what is indeed a doctrine of the incarnation whose success in avoiding outright heresy is therefore more than merely verbal. Be this as it may, the main point is simply that where traditional incarnational doctrine clearly has been more than merely verbal, it has usually run into the difficulty of implicitly denying the true humanity of Jesus Christ.

Having commented on these three difficulties of the traditional doctrine of the incarnation, I should perhaps explain that my purpose in doing so is in no way to refute the position of those who would still defend it. Anyone acquainted with theological discussion knows that every position has its difficulties and that hardly any position's difficulties can be so great as to render it incapable of defense by those who are concerned and resourceful enough to defend it. Certainly the subtle defenses of the doctrine of the incarnation by several contemporary theologians could not possibly be justly disposed of except by the closest kind of criticism and counterargument. But each of us must continually decide where his or her own theological resources are best employed; and critical for this decision, in my opinion, is an assessment of the relative difficulties of the positions between which one may reasonably be required to choose in the given situation. Where the difficulties continue to appear considerable and more or less intractable, one has sufficient reason to continue exploring other options whose difficulties seem comparatively minor and more amenable to resolution. Accordingly, my purpose in discussing the difficulties of traditional incarnational doctrine, as well as the other main reason I find traditional christology problematic, is simply to make clear why, like a great number of my contemporaries, I continue to explore the alternative of a revisionary christology.

This discussion also serves, of course, to indicate at least negatively the aims that such a revisionary christology itself must be concerned to achieve. First of all and fundamentally, it must be concerned to so formulate the point of the christology of witness as to demythologize it consistently and without remainder. By this I do not imply, any more than Bultmann ever did, that mythological concepts and symbols are simply an antiquated form of thinking and speaking no longer having any place in witness and theology. The purpose of demythologizing, as Bultmann never tired of insisting, is not to *eliminate* mythology but to *interpret* it, which is to say, to recognize it for the kind of thinking and speaking it really is, and hence to recognize that the truth it expresses, insofar as it does so, is very different from a strictly empirical kind of truth. One reason such demythologizing is imperative has already been discussed: it is the only way the christology of witness can be made to seem credible or even relevant to persons sharing a modern picture of the world and understanding of themselves. But there is the further reason that one can recognize mythology as the kind of thinking and speaking it really is only by also recognizing that its empirical terms and categories are finally inappropriate to the nonempirical truth it attempts to express. In other words, thoroughgoing demythologizing, as Bultmann himself rightly argues, is also a demand of faith itself, insofar as the point of the christology of witness can be made appropriately as well as credibly only by being interpreted in nonmythological terms (Bultmann, 1952b: 207–208).

But any interpretation obviously requires an *interpretans* as well as an *interpretandum;* and so the second thing a revisionary christology must be concerned with is providing an alternative conceptuality and symbolism in terms of which the point of christology can be made appropriately as well as credibly. If there are good reasons for holding that any such conceptuality and symbolism must in the last analysis be metaphysical, there are also reasons, as we have seen, for insisting that the metaphysics in question ought not to be the classical metaphysics presupposed by the traditional doctrine of the incarnation. Not only is this classical metaphysics hardly credible to us today, given our own experience and critical reflection, but it is also doubtfully appropriate for talking about God, self, and the world so as to express the necessary implications of the christology of witness whose point theology is supposed to make. Moreover, it is arguable that the same classical metaphysical assumptions account for the other principal difficulties we have observed in traditional incarnational doctrine—namely, that its attempts to avoid the apparent self-contradiction that Jesus the Christ is both God and man have proved to be either merely verbal, lacking assignable conceptual meaning, or else one form or other of heresy, most commonly the heresy of denying that Jesus is truly human. In any event, a christology would not be sufficiently revisionary unless, in addition to providing concepts and symbols in which to make the point of christology at once credibly and appropriately, it so formulated this point as to really say something, avoiding both self-contradiction and mere verbiage as well as any implication that Jesus was somehow less than a fully human being.

But as I implied earlier, some such aims as these, which any number of theologians today are committed to somehow achieving, have been the aims of an ever growing minority of Christian theologians at least since Schleiermacher (Faut: 2–63; Grass, 1973: 93–99). Furthermore, during the time in

which these aims have been actively pursued, several christologies have been produced for the express purpose of realizing the project of such a revisionary christology. As one
would expect, these several christologies have differed from
one another in important respects, even in basic approach
and method and above all in what they could reasonably
assume concerning the use of the New Testament writings as
empirical-historical sources and in the metaphysics or other
conceptuality and symbolism in terms of which they have
attempted to make the point of christology. Also, there has
understandably been a significant difference between the
revisionary christologies typically developed by Protestant
theologians from Schleiermacher on and those typically developed more recently by Roman Catholics, especially since
the Second Vatican Council. Whereas the Protestant christologies have usually aimed at replacing traditional christology with an understanding of Christ held to be at once
more scriptural and more contemporary, their Catholic
counterparts, except perhaps for those developed by the earlier Modernists and some appearing most recently, have
taken for granted that dogma can be revised forwards but
never backwards and so have aimed only to reformulate
traditional christology, not to replace it.

But as significant as this and all the other differences between them certainly are, there are also important respects
in which the several revisionary christologies, earlier and
more recent, Catholic as well as Protestant, all tend to be
very much alike. And the really crucial thing to note, so far
as the argument of this book is concerned, is that the important respects in which most of them are similar are by no
means limited to what we have previously identified as the
aims of a revisionary christology. On the contrary, judging
from the repeated attempts already made to achieve these
aims, one must allow that there are certain other characteristics that are every bit as essential to defining by far most

christologies of a revisionary type, if not indeed this type of christology itself.

Because this is so, however, I find it necessary to speak of the *problem* of a revisionary christology. In my opinion, these other characteristics that have so far proved to define most christologies with revisionary aims make them hardly less problematic than the traditional christology they have sought to revise. In fact, as confident as I am of the aims of revisionary christology, I am just as certain that these other defining characteristics of most actual revisionary christologies make it quite impossible to achieve their aims by formulating the witness to Christ at once appropriately and credibly in our present situation. Thus, as I see it, if one can make the point of christology today only by also talking about it, this is doubly so: not only because traditional christology is problematic, but because the same is true of revisionary christology as well, at least as represented by most of the attempts so far made to achieve its aims. The specific problem this book is an attempt to solve, then, is whether there can be such a thing as a revisionary christology that is not problematic in this same way and, therefore, is sufficiently different from most other revisionary christologies to achieve the aims that they have till now proved incapable of achieving.

Exactly what this means can be made clear only in the course of succeeding chapters. But we need at least a general idea of what lies ahead of us, and this we can acquire by briefly considering the characteristics of revisionary christologies that, as I shall be arguing, make most of them inadequate, given the limits and opportunities of our situation today. Because the characteristics in question are all characteristics of what amounts to a contemporary consensus among revisionary theologians, I shall speak of them henceforth as the specific points in such a consensus.

It should not be inferred from this, however, that revisionary theologians are alone in now being generally agreed about any or even all of these points. One of the common characteristics of revisionary movements generally is that they tend to exhibit more extensive agreement with the traditional positions of which they are revisions than persons on either side are likely to realize. Thus, even if they do not agree in giving the same answer, they nevertheless do agree in asking the same question. This, as we shall see, has certainly been borne out by the revisionary christologies whose way of asking the question of christology is not really different from that of traditional christology, however different their way of answering it. Or, again, it commonly happens that the longer a traditional position continues to be confronted by a revisionary alternative, the more it tends to acquire certain revisionary characteristics, even those that at first were most challenging. Here too the developments in modern christology conform to a common pattern. For if the so-called quest of the historical Jesus began as one of the most challenging of revisionary projects, some of the most committed contemporary questers are to be found among those who still seek to defend traditional christology.

There are various reasons, then, why specific points in the contemporary revisionary consensus, if not the consensus itself, are matters of general agreement well beyond the ranks of revisionary theologians. But, whatever the extent of the agreement about them, there are clearly certain things that most revisionary theologians today take to be essential to an adequate christology; and I maintain that it is the consensus thereby established that makes the point of christology for us not singly but doubly problematic.

There are, as I see it, three specific points in this consensus, each of which is more or less closely related to the other two.

In the first place, revisionary theologians are generally agreed that the question christology properly asks and answers is the question "Who is Jesus?" understood as asking about the being of Jesus in himself, as distinct from asking about the meaning of Jesus for us. Actually, to say that revisionary theologians are now generally agreed about this may be misleading if it is taken to mean that, having fully considered the question, they have deliberately taken this position instead of some possible alternative. The fact of the matter is that they typically show as little interest as their traditional counterparts in asking the logically prior question of the question of christology, and hence they tend to answer it merely by assumption as distinct from full consideration of the relevant alternatives and deliberate decision between them. It is not at all surprising, then, that, as I already noted, their way of asking the christological question is not really different from that of traditional theologians. For them too the question of christology is still asked as a question of explanation, where the *explanandum* is simply the person of Jesus who is said to be Christ, and the *explanans,* some hypothesis about the nature of this person, his qualities, his mode of being, his relation to God, and so on. Thus, while revisionary theologians may no longer think and speak of Jesus as uniquely God in man, they do typically think and speak of him as uniquely man of God; and however different this may be as an answer to the christological question, one can hardly fail to recognize that the question itself remains the same. It is still the question about the identity of Jesus in himself, asked and answered independently of any question about the identity of the person who asks it or of the ultimate reality with which he or she has to do.

A second point of general agreement is by way of formally identifying this Jesus who is the subject of the christological question, and hence of any assertion that can possibly answer it. According to the position typically taken in revisionary christologies, the Jesus who is said to be Christ is formally identified as none other than the so-called historical Jesus, in the sense of the actual Jesus of history insofar as he can be known to us today by way of empirical-historical inquiry using the writings of the New Testament as sources (Harvey, 1966: 265 ff.). It is for this reason that revisionary theologians today usually argue for the historical possibility as well as the theological necessity of a quest of the historical Jesus, which, as we saw earlier, began as a project of revisionary christology. They do so, of course, in a situation that has vastly changed since the quest first began as regards what may be reasonably assumed about the use of the New Testament writings as sources of empirical-historical knowledge about Jesus. But even if they are quite prepared to allow that an older quest of the historical Jesus is as impossible historically as it is unnecessary theologically, they nevertheless contend that, insofar as it is the actual Jesus of history who is asserted to be the Christ, we both can and must know enough about him as a figure of the past to justify this assertion.

The third point in the revisionary consensus also has to do with justifying this assertion, although the reference here is not to the subject of the assertion but to its predicate. If this assertion is justified, in that Jesus is truthfully said to be Christ, this can only be because any conditions necessary for truthfully asserting the predicate "the Christ" of any subject are, in fact, satisfied by the particular subject Jesus. But this raises the question of the conditions of truthful predication necessarily implied by this as well as any other christological predicate. And to this question the answer typically given in revisionary christologies is that Jesus can be truthfully said to be Christ if, but only if, he himself, as a human person, perfectly actualized the possibility of authentic self-understanding. In other words, Jesus is the Christ because, as I already expressed it in discussing the first point in the consensus, he was uniquely man of God, uniquely a man whose openness to the gift and demand of God in his own personal life was such that God was as fully immanent in him as it is possible for God to be in any human person. Of course, traditional christology, also, has made a claim for the perfection of Jesus' human life by asserting his sinlessness, as, for example, in the assertion of the Chalcedonian definition that he is "coessential with us . . . as to his humanity, being like us in every respect apart from sin" (Norris [ed.]: 159). But whereas for traditional christology this claim is implied by the incarnation, by Jesus' being also and primarily uniquely God in man, for revisionary christologies the claim for Jesus' human perfection stands alone. One might even say, in fact, that it is so far from being the effect of the incarnation as to be its cause, in the sense that it expresses not only a necessary but the sufficient condition of asserting any christological predicate and hence also justifies asserting that God was incarnate in Jesus in whatever sense this can still be asserted.

Now, as I have said, all three of these points are sufficiently problematic to create the special problem of a revisionary christology. Consequently, one task in the chapters to follow is to take up each of the points in turn to determine whether there is not some alternative possible answer to the same question that is not similarly problematic. My conviction, obviously, is that such alternative answers are indeed possible and that, taken together, they provide a way of talking about the point of christology that is fully consistent with revisionary aims, even while being considerably more adequate in our situation today than the way in which most of the christologies pursuing these aims have talked about it. But whether or to what extent this conviction is well founded can be determined only by the argument of succeeding chapters.

In any event, as necessary and important as it is to talk about the point of christology and to do so adequately, it is neither the only nor even the primary task of a contemporary christology of reflection. Rather, its primary task, and hence our other, principal task in this book, is actually to make the point of the christology of witness in a way that will be at once appropriate to this witness itself and credible to men and women today. Of course, this too is clearly a relative, not an absolute distinction. Talking about the point of christology is already a way, however indirect, of making it, even as making the point of christology, at least as a christology of reflection has to make it, is still only a way of talking about it. Because this is so, the difference between the two main parts of the book—the one part comprising Chapters 1 through 4, the other Chapters 5 through 8—is at best a relative difference. Although each part has its distinctive task in the overall argument, it unavoidably overlaps with the other and presupposes the other for its completion.

2. The Question Christology Answers

The point of christology, I have argued, has now become sufficiently problematic that one can make it only by also talking about it. In fact, the point of the christology of witness is now doubly problematic: not only because the traditional christology based on scripture and dogma has long since become a serious problem but also because the same is now true of most of the revisionary christologies so far developed to replace or reformulate it. Consequently, even if one is committed, as I am, to revisionary aims, one still has to face what I have called "the problem of a revisionary christology," which is to say, the problem of replacing an untenable consensus among contemporary revisionary theologians about the point of christology with a way of talking about its point that is not similarly untenable. Thus, if our constructive task in this book is to make the point of christology in terms adequate to our situation today, our critical task is to talk about its point in a way that is likewise appropriate and credible.

It is this critical task that I propose to take up in the present chapter, by considering further the first point in the contemporary revisionary consensus. This point, it will be recalled, is the answer revisionary theologians are now generally agreed in assuming to the question concerning the question of christology or the question christology answers. Before explaining why this seems to me to be the proper point at which to begin the critical part of my argument, I need to elaborate somewhat on what I have already said about the

meaning of the word "christology," so as to clarify a phrase
of which I shall henceforth make a good deal of use—namely,
"the constitutive christological assertion."

If in its obvious literal sense "christology" means *logos*
about *christos,* or thought and speech about Christ, it has
long since come to be used much more broadly for any
thought and speech about Jesus who is said to be Christ, even
where the witness borne to him may not be formulated in
terms of this particular honorific title. Thus no one would
hesitate to speak of a particular witness as christology simply
because it thought and spoke about Jesus not as Christ, but
as the Son of Man, the Lord, the Son of God, or in terms of
one of the many other titles that Christians have used in
bearing witness to him. Furthermore, it is readily apparent
from the New Testament and the creeds of the church that
predicating such honorific titles of Jesus is by no means the
only way in which Christians have formulated their witness
to him anyhow. There are also the different, if closely related,
formulations in which they have expressed Jesus' decisive
significance for human existence by making what we can
think of only as mythological or legendary assertions about
his origin and destiny or the course of his life. So, in the
second article of the Apostles' Creed, for instance, these two
kinds of christological formulation are combined—the initial
and presumably older assertion in terms of titles that Jesus is
the Christ, God's only Son, our Lord, being qualified by a
series of relative clauses asserting his unique origin and destiny, such as that he was conceived by the Holy Spirit and
born of the Virgin Mary and that the third day he rose from
the dead and ascended into heaven (Kelly: 139–152). Clearly,
all such assertions about Jesus, whether of the one kind or of
the other, are logically of a piece, and so it is only fitting that
they should all be taken as belonging to the thought and
speech that the word "christology" is ordinarily understood
to cover.

Because this is fitting, however, it seems equally fitting to
speak of the constitutive christological assertion, meaning
thereby the assertion about Jesus, however formulated, that
constitutes christology explicitly as such. Of course, this constitutive assertion of christology cannot be made at all except
in some formulation or other—if not in traditional terms of
honorific titles or mythological and legendary claims, then in
some other terms. But as essential as it is to realize this, it in
no way obviates distinguishing between the constitutive
christological assertion itself and any particular christological
formulation that makes or implies it. All such formulations
are evidently only different ways of making or implying one
and the same assertion, and it is with this assertion that a
christology of reflection always has to do both in critically
interpreting the christology of witness and in formulating
this witness in and for its own situation. With this in mind, I
shall henceforth speak of the constitutive christological assertion—or, more concisely, of the christological assertion—in
many places where my usage up to now would have allowed
me to speak simply of christology. In this way, I hope to
introduce a certain precision into the discussion, whose ad-
vantages should become apparent as the argument proceeds.

The question now before us, I have said, is a question about
a question—specifically, the question answered by christology, or, as we may now say more precisely, by the constitutive christological assertion. This would be the proper place
to begin our inquiry in any case, because whenever one is
uncertain about the point of any assertion, asking about the
question it answers always has logical priority. We grasp the
meaning of an assertion and can affirm its truth only when we
understand the question it is intended to answer. But if this
is true of assertions generally, there are special reasons for
recognizing its truth in the case of the christological assertion.

One such reason already appeared in the opening chapter
when I pointed out that, for all of the differences between

their respective answers, traditional and revisionary christologies are agreed in asking essentially the same question.
For both types of christology, the question answered by the
constitutive christological assertion is the question "Who is
Jesus?" taken as asking about the being of Jesus in himself
rather than about the meaning of Jesus for us. If such extensive agreement about the question of christology may seem
at first glance to make inquiring about it unnecessary, one
needs to recall what Alfred North Whitehead speaks of as
"the old advice that the doctrines which best repay critical
examination are those which for the longest period have
remained unquestioned" (Whitehead, 1933: 228). Clearly, the
one thing in conventional christological discussion that is
certain to have remained unquestioned the longest is the
way of asking the christological question that both traditional
and revisionary ways of answering it necessarily presuppose.
But if this is already additional justification for asking about
the christological question, there is yet another reason for
doing so. Notwithstanding the extent of the conventional
agreement about it, there are important indications that the
question the christological assertion answers is a very different kind of question. This may be brought out by considering
some explicit christological formulations from the New Testament.

Consider, first, the confession of Peter in Matthew 16, to
which I made reference at the beginning of the book. "You
are the Christ, the Son of the living God," Peter affirms, in
direct response to Jesus' question to the disciples, "But who
do you say that I am?" (vv. 15 f.). On the face of it, one would
appear justified in inferring that the christological question
presupposed here is indeed simply "Who is Jesus?" Because
Jesus is evidently the subject of the assertion implied by
Peter's confession, it surely must be he about whom the
question asks, to which this assertion expresses an answer.

And yet even here there are indications that this obvious
inference may be rather too simple. For one thing, Peter's

response is a personal confession and therefore *implies* the christological assertion rather than actually makes it. But if it could hardly be anything else and still be a proper response to Jesus' question, this question itself evidently presupposes that there can be assertions about Jesus other than the christological assertion. The context makes clear that if Peter, representing the disciples, implies that Jesus is the Christ, the Son of the living God, some men assert, on the contrary, that he is John the Baptist, others, that he is Elijah, and yet others, that he is Jeremiah or one of the prophets (v. 14). In other words, the passage indicates that answers to the question of who Jesus is are strictly correlated with answers to another question about who the different persons are who give these different answers (Marxsen, 1969: 214–225). Of course, the clear implication of the whole passage is that there is the further important difference between the answers, that not all of them are true, as one of them certainly is. This is clear enough from Jesus' assurance that it is not flesh and blood that has revealed his identity to Peter, but rather his Father who is in heaven (v. 17). But if the passage as a whole thus serves to bear witness that Jesus really is who Peter confesses him to be, it also serves to authorize the existence of Peter, the representative disciple, as authentic human existence. Because of his confession, indeed, Peter is the rock on which Jesus will build the church that the powers of death shall never conquer, and he will be given the keys of the kingdom of heaven (vv. 18 f.).

If even this passage indicates that the conventional understanding of the question of christology may be too simple, other formulations leave little doubt about it. This is particularly true of the christology developed in the Fourth Gospel. In John 1:18, for instance, we read, "No one has ever seen God; the only Son, who is in the bosom of the Father, he has made him known." By implication, Jesus is here asserted to be the only Son from the Father (cf. 1:14), and this assertion is evidently connected with the claim—whether as ground or as consequence—that he reveals the God whom no one has ever seen precisely as his Father. But this means that the question presupposed by this assertion is not only, or even primarily, "Who is Jesus?" If God is indeed the unseen God whom Jesus makes known, then also presupposed in asserting that he is the only Son is the prior question "Who is God?" This question is prior in the strictly logical sense that, unless it had already been asked, the question "Who is Jesus?" would not even have arisen, at least in the sense presupposed by the assertion that he is the only Son. Because the question "Who is God?" is thus logically prior, however, this assertion in effect has two subjects, not merely one. It not only identifies Jesus as the only Son of God but, at one and the same time, also identifies the only true God as the Father of Jesus.

The soundness of this interpretation is confirmed by other christological formulations characteristic of the Fourth Gospel. Striking in this respect are the so-called "I am" sayings, which include such familiar claims of Jesus as the following:

> I am the bread of life; he who comes to me shall not hunger, and he who believes in me shall never thirst (6:35).

> I am the light of the world; he who follows me will not walk in darkness, but will have the light of life (8:12).

> I am the door; if any one enters by me, he will be saved, and will go in and out and find pasture (10:9).

> I am the good shepherd (10:11, 14).

> I am the resurrection and the life; he who believes in me, though he die, yet shall he live, and whoever lives and believes in me shall never die (11:25 f.).

> I am the way, and the truth, and the life; no one comes to the Father, but by me (14:6).

> I am the true vine (15:1, 5).

Translated in this way, each of these claims appears to imply a particular formulation of the christological assertion, such as "Jesus is the bread of life," "Jesus is the light of the world," and so on. For this reason, one could infer that the question they all presuppose is simply the question "Who is Jesus?" But as students of Greek well know, there is no change in the person of the verb between "I *am* he" and "It *is* I," both of these English statements translating the same two Greek words, ἐγώ εἰμι. Consequently, the only way to determine which statement is required to translate the intended meaning in a particular case is to consider the context.

Significantly, careful interpreters of the Fourth Gospel have concluded that the word ἐγώ in these sayings is really a predicate rather than a subject, which means that they are properly translated differently from the Revised Standard Version translation previously cited. Instead of "I am the bread of life," one properly translates, "The bread of life— it is I" (Bultmann, 1953: 167 f., n.2; 1965: 379, 417; Brown, 1966: 533–538). This means, then, that the christological assertion implied by this claim must be reformulated accordingly to read not "Jesus is the bread of life," but rather "The bread of life—it is Jesus," whereupon it at once becomes clear that the question presupposed by the assertion cannot be simply "Who is Jesus?" On the contrary, the question the assertion most obviously answers is "Who or what is the bread of life?"

If we ask now what kind of a question this is, the answer seems clear enough. To ask about the bread of life, or the light of the world, or any of the other things that figure in these sayings, is evidently to ask about that reality upon which one knows oneself to be ultimately dependent if one is to realize one's human existence in the emphatic sense of authentic existence. This assumes that being human, one can never simply live one's life as a plant or an animal can but must always somehow lead it, and that one can lead it only by understanding it. Thus, when one asks for the light of the world, say, one asks for that understanding of one's existence and of the ultimate reality on which it depends that is the true or authentic understanding, as over against all the misunderstandings that leave one to walk only in darkness. Presupposing this question, then, Jesus' claim that the light of the world is he asserts in effect that the authentic self-understanding that human beings need and ask for simply because they are human is explicitly offered to them through him, in the understanding of their existence to which he himself calls them.

That this assertion in context is indeed intended to assert something about Jesus is beyond question. It is precisely he and no one else through whom the authentic self-understanding for which all persons are asking is explicitly authorized; and this is underscored when he is said to be "the *true* light" (1:9; cf. 1 John 2:8), even as he himself claims that it is he who is "the *true* bread," "the *true* vine," and "the *good* shepherd"—all of these being equivalent ways of talking about what is ultimately true and real as over against all that is false and merely apparent. And yet as certain as it is that the assertion implied by all these formulations is indeed intended to assert who Jesus is, it is every bit as certain that this is not the only question it is intended to answer. Because Jesus is the predicate rather than the subject of the assertion, it is also intended, at one and the same time, to answer the question of who we ourselves are—by asserting, namely, that ultimate reality and, therefore, our own authentic existence as men and women are none other than they are disclosed to us to be precisely through Jesus.

The import of these considerations should now be clear. Insofar as one may judge from the small sample of New Testament christology that we have considered, one has good reason to challenge the adequacy of the conventional understanding of the christological question. This is not to say, naturally, that there is something wrong with what the conventional understanding affirms. Without a doubt the question christology answers *is* the question "Who is Jesus?" But what certainly is wrong in this understanding is what it in effect denies in assuming that this is the *only* question christology answers. The formulations we have considered make perfectly clear that there are two other questions to which the christological assertion is also intended to give an answer at the same time that it is intended to assert who Jesus is. On the one hand, there is the question "Who is God?" understood as asking about the ultimate reality upon which we are each dependent for our own being and meaning as human persons. On the other hand, there is the question "Who are we?" or better, "Who am I?" which we are each led to ask more or less explicitly insofar as we are concerned not to miss but to attain our own authentic existence as human beings. That both of these questions too are necessarily asked in asking who Jesus is is particularly apparent from the formulations we have considered from the Fourth Gospel. But even in the case of Matthew 16, it is evident upon reflection that Jesus' question "But who do you say that I am?" is not simple but complex. Calling as it does for a personal confession, and a confession, moreover, that can be made only by the revelation of God, it confronts me with the same three questions: not only who Jesus is but also, and inescapably, who I am and who God is (Schmithals: 181 f.).

My contention is that a larger sample of New Testament christology would tend only to confirm this essential complexity of the christological question (Bultmann, 1952a: 252 f.). Certainly, in the places in the New Testament where one finds what Leslie Houlden calls "the creed of experience," which is to say, christological formulations that are in close touch with the earliest experience of Jesus in the Christian community, one has no difficulty showing that all three of the questions that we have analyzed are presupposed (Hick [ed.]: 125–132).

But if I am right about this, the fallacy involved in the first point of the revisionary consensus is obvious. It is a special case of what Whitehead calls, in a characteristically apt phrase, "the fallacy of misplaced concreteness." By this he means the mistake one always makes when one treats what is but an abstract aspect of some larger concrete whole as though it were the whole itself, or at any rate something concrete (Whitehead, 1925: 74 ff., 84 ff.). Simply to assume, as revisionary theologians continue to do, that the only question the christological assertion answers is "Who is Jesus?" is to make this very mistake. For it is to treat what is but one abstract aspect of the christological question as though it were the whole concrete question, or at least a concrete question independent of the other aspects. The result is that even the one aspect that is mistaken for a concrete question becomes very different from what it is in its actual context together with the other aspects. Instead of being the question about the meaning of Jesus for us, given the logically prior questions about the meaning of our own existence and about the ultimate reality by which our existence is determined, it becomes the very different question about the being of Jesus in himself, about *his* existence as determined by ultimate reality, and so on.

In other words, these other two aspects of the christological question are not only essential to it, they are also fundamental to its third aspect. For unless one were already asking about one's own identity and the identity of the mysterious ultimate reality upon which one's being and meaning are dependent, one neither would nor could ask the question "Who is Jesus?" in the distinctive sense in which it is asked in asking the question of christology.

Recognizing this, we need to inquire further about these other logically prior questions that are the more fundamental aspects of the question christology answers. Just what kind of questions are they, and how, exactly, are they related?

The answer I shall argue for is that they are not so much two questions as two essential aspects of one question—the question I call "the existential question," or alternatively "the question of faith." I speak of it as "the existential question," because, as we shall see, it has to do with the ultimate meaning of one's very existence as a human being and, therefore, is and must be asked at least implicitly by anyone who exists humanly at all. Alternatively I call it "the question of faith" insofar as I advert to the "basic supposition" underlying it (Christian: 84–88). Like any other question, it is possible at all only because or insofar as in asking it one supposes certain things to be the case. But in asking this question, what one necessarily supposes to be the case is what is perforce supposed by our basic faith simply as human beings in the ultimate meaning of our lives—namely, that our own existence and all existence are somehow justified or worthwhile and that, therefore, ultimate reality is such as to authorize some understanding of ourselves as authentic, just as, conversely, there is some understanding of our existence that is authentic because it is the self-understanding authorized by ultimate reality. As far as I can see, at least this much in the way of faith is basic to our very existence as human beings, because it is at least implicitly presupposed as the necessary condition of the possibility of all that we think or say or do (Ogden, 1971: 55–59; 1977: 21–43, 120–143). But if this is correct, such basic faith in the worth of life is the underlying supposition of the existential question presupposed by christology, and it is this to which I intend to call attention by also speaking of this question as "the question of faith."

This same question may also be called "the religious question," assuming, as I do, that what is properly meant by "religion" is the primary form of culture in which the existential question, or the question of faith, is explicitly asked and answered (Ogden, 1978: 6–10). As I have said, this question is and must be asked implicitly insofar as we exist humanly at all; and because the basic faith underlying it is a necessary condition of whatever we think or say or do, some answer to it is necessarily implied by all the forms of culture, secular as well as religious. The distinctive thing about religion, however, is that it not only implies an answer to the existential question but also explicates such an answer, just this being its unique function as a primary form of culture alongside the other, secular forms. But if this means that the existential question is indeed the religious question insofar as it is asked and answered explicitly, it also means that it is by the analysis of religion above all that one can discern the essential logical structure of the existential question. With this in mind, I should now like to appeal to just such an analysis to support the understanding of this question for which I shall be arguing.

The analysis to which I refer is that of the anthropologist Clifford Geertz, who has set forth a comprehensive understanding of religion in several essays elaborating what he calls "a semiotic concept of culture" (Geertz: 29). No doubt the most systematic as well as the best known of these essays is "Religion as a Cultural System," in which Geertz characterizes religion as a system of "sacred symbols," and hence as a specific form of "culture," by which he understands in general "a system of inherited conceptions expressed in symbolic forms by means of which men communicate, perpetuate, and develop their knowledge about and attitudes toward life" (89). For our purposes here, however, another essay, entitled "Ethos, World View, and the Analysis of Sacred Symbols," provides a more relevant statement of the same understanding.

According to Geertz, "the view of man as a symbolizing, conceptualizing, meaning-seeking animal" opens up "a whole new approach" to the analysis of religion. Because "the drive to make sense out of experience, to give it form and order, is evidently as real and as pressing as the more familiar biological needs," religion can and should be interpreted as an attempt "to provide orientation for an organism which cannot live in a world it is unable to understand." As such, "religion is never merely metaphysics," because "the holy bears within it everywhere a sense of intrinsic obligation: it not only encourages devotion, it demands it; it not only induces intellectual assent, it enforces emotional commitment." On the other hand, "never merely metaphysics, religion is never merely ethics either"; for "the source of its moral vitality is conceived to lie in the fidelity with which it expresses the fundamental nature of reality. The powerfully coercive 'ought' is felt to grow out of a comprehensive factual 'is,' and in such a way religion grounds the most specific requirements of human action in the most general contexts of human existence" (140 f., 126).

On Geertz's analysis, then, religion as a specific kind of symbolism is a "synthesis," or "fusion," having two "sides" or "aspects," which he refers to respectively as "ethos" and "world view." The first comprises the "evaluative," or "normative," elements of a given culture, and thus "the underlying attitude toward themselves and their world" that the life of a people reflects, while the second comprises the "cognitive," or "existential," elements expressed in "their picture of the way things in sheer actuality are, their concept of nature, of self, of society." By means of the synthesis that religion effects, "the ethos is made intellectually reasonable by being shown to represent a way of life implied by the actual state of affairs which the world view describes, and the world view is made emotionally acceptable by being presented as an image of an actual state of affairs of which such a way of life is an authentic expression" (126 f.).

If this formulation appears to imply that the two essential aspects of religion are equally fundamental, this impression is further confirmed by other formulations expressing symmetry between them—as when Geertz says that, as a result of religion, "between the approved style of life and the assumed structure of reality there is conceived to be a simple and fundamental congruence such that they complete one another and lend one another meaning" (129). But there are yet other formulations that clearly seem to express a certain asymmetry between the two aspects, insofar as ethos is made to depend on world view in a way in which world view hardly depends on ethos.

Thus Geertz avers that "what all sacred symbols assert is that the good for man is to live realistically; where they differ is in the vision of reality they construct." Were world view and ethos equally fundamental, Geertz would presumably not explain the difference between sacred symbols solely by reference to the first. And one feels confirmed in this conclusion insofar as the need that Geertz sees religion meeting is above all the need for "a metaphysical grounding for values." Although he expressly insists that "the relation between ethos and world view is circular," and thus allows for drawing "factual conclusions from normative premises" as well as "normative conclusions from factual premises," it is clearly the second kind of inference that he singles out when he says that for religion the "ought" is felt to grow out of an "is." "However its role may differ at various times, for various individuals, and in various cultures, religion, by fusing ethos and world view, gives to a set of social values what they perhaps most need to be coercive: an appearance of objectivity. In sacred rituals and myths values are portrayed not as subjective human preferences but as the imposed conditions for life implicit in a world with a particular structure" (130, 141, 131).

I should not want to make too much of the point that Geertz's analysis of religion allows for a certain priority of world view to ethos, even though both aspects are essential. Clearly, what stands out in his analysis is that religion is neither merely metaphysics nor merely ethics but, in Schleiermacher's phrase, "the necessary and indispensable third," which is distinct from the one as well as the other even while having aspects that closely relate it to both

(Schleiermacher, 1967: 50). Insofar as the way of life religion commends is understood to be an authentic expression of its vision of ultimate reality, its aspect of ethos is evidently grounded in its aspect of world view. But while religion thus definitely functions to provide a metaphysical foundation for morals, it also functions, conversely, to express the moral meaning of the metaphysical. Thus Geertz can also stress that the "peculiar power" of sacred symbols "comes from their presumed ability to identify fact with value at the most fundamental level, to give to what is otherwise merely actual, a comprehensive normative import" (Geertz: 127).

On the assumption now that it is by religion in this sense that the existential question is explicitly asked and answered, what can we discern as to the logical structure of this question? Presumably its structure is that of a single question that is neither merely metaphysical nor merely moral but distinct from both, even while having aspects that respectively relate it to each. Accordingly, it can be described as the question about the meaning of ultimate reality for us, which asks at one and the same time about both ultimate reality and ourselves: both the ultimate reality that authorizes an authentic understanding of our own existence and the authentic self-understanding that is authorized by what is ultimately real.

As such, the existential question has, on the one hand, a *metaphysical* aspect in which it is distinct from all properly metaphysical questions, even while being closely related to them. It is distinct from such questions insofar as it asks about the meaning of ultimate reality for us, while they ask about the structure of ultimate reality in itself. But it is also closely related to such questions insofar as any answer to it necessarily implies certain answers to them. This is so because it is only insofar as ultimate reality in itself has one structure rather than another that it can have the meaning for us it is asserted to have in taking it to authorize one self-understanding rather than another as the authentic understanding of ourselves. On the other hand, the existential question has a *moral* aspect in which it is both distinct from and closely related to all properly moral questions. It is distinct from moral questions insofar as it asks about the authentic understanding of our existence authorized by ultimate reality, while they ask about how one is to act in relation to one's fellow beings. But it is also closely related to such questions insofar as any answer to it has certain necessary implications for any answers to them. This is the case because it is only insofar as acting in one way rather than another is how one ought to act in relation to one's fellows that ultimate reality can have the meaning for us it is asserted to have in taking it to authorize one self-understanding rather than another as authentic.

Of course, as thus analyzed the existential question might be said to be two questions rather than one, insofar as, in asking it, one asks about both ultimate reality and authentic self-understanding. But as true as this certainly is, it should be clear from what has been said that there is an overlap between the two questions that speaking of them simply as two fails adequately to take into account. In asking about the meaning of ultimate reality for us, one asks about ultimate reality only insofar as it authorizes authentic self-understanding, even as one asks about authentic self-understanding only insofar as it is authorized by ultimate reality. Recognizing this, I prefer to speak of the existential question neither simply as two questions nor simply as one question, but rather as one question with two essential aspects, metaphysical and moral, each of which necessarily implies the other.

But what reason is there to suppose that this is the question that accounts for the more fundamental aspects of the question answered by the christological assertion? To judge from the examples of New Testament christology that we considered earlier, one is surely justified in claiming that the logically prior question they presuppose is not a vague, general

question about the meaning of *ultimate reality* for us, but
rather the definite, quite specific question about the meaning
of *God* for us. Thus, to recall one such example, we saw that
it is precisely the question "Who is God?" that is evidently
presupposed by the Johannine formulation "No one has ever
seen God; the only Son, who is in the bosom of the Father,
he has made him known." To be sure, we also noted that it
is of what is ultimately true and real that the Fourth Gospel
intends to speak by such obviously symbolic terms as "the
bread of life," "the light of the world," and so on. But if we
keep in mind the explicitly theistic structure of Johannine
christology, there can be no doubt that what it assumes to be
ultimately true and real is precisely God and that it is therefore God, or what decisively re-presents God, of which all
such terms are intended to be symbols.

Indeed so, and I should not think of suggesting that the
question answered not only by Johannine christology but by
all the christologies in the New Testament could be anything
except explicitly theistic in its most fundamental aspect. Still
I am concerned to make clear that the question about God
that these christologies all seek to answer is the properly
religious question about the meaning of God for us, not the
properly *metaphysical* question about the structure of God
in itself—although, naturally, this second question is necessarily implied by the first, for the reasons I have just explained. I am presupposing, obviously, that the term "God"
is systematically ambiguous insofar as it can function in a
metaphysical as well as a religious context of meaning with
a significantly different sense depending on its context. But
this presupposition seems warranted insofar as "God" clearly
functions in asking the question answered by christology
with a religious rather than a metaphysical sense, in that it
is one way—specifically, the theistic religious way—of explicitly thinking and speaking about ultimate reality as authorizing authentic human existence.

In other words, if religion generally can be defined as the form of culture in which the existential question of the meaning of ultimate reality for us is explicitly asked and answered, theistic religion in particular can be defined as the specific way of explicitly asking and answering this question whose constitutive concept and symbol is "God." Far from in any way suggesting, then, that the question christology answers is other than the specifically theistic question "Who is God?" I have been concerned to clarify what it means to ask this very question in the properly religious sense in which the christological assertion answers it.

The distinctive thing about theistic religions, of course, is that the meaning of God for us is just what they take to be in question. Although the whole point of the term "God," so far as its properly religious meaning is concerned, is to explicitly identify ultimate reality in a certain way as authorizing authentic self-understanding, different theistic religions, all of which are formally the same in thus making use of the term, nevertheless represent understandings of the meaning of ultimate reality for us that are materially different. Who God is and who we are therefore given and called to be in relation to God are understood in one way here, in another, very different way there. The result is that the same term that functions in one respect to *answer* the existential question can function in another respect only to *ask* it, the meaning of God for us having become the very thing that is in question.

This explains in part, certainly, why it is also characteristic of theistic religions that they each develop certain other concepts and symbols, the whole point of which is to answer their question about who God is by explicitly identifying someone or something that decisively re-presents God. Once the identity of God has become questionable, the theistic way of asking and answering the existential question is thus to focus on some decisive re-presentation of God, whereby the meaning of God for us is itself made fully explicit. The concepts and symbols that are actually developed for this purpose naturally cover an immense range of differences if one mistakenly regards them merely as metaphysical. According to some of them, the decisive re-presentation of God is some abstract aspect of God's own being, such as God's "Wisdom" or "Word," say, while for others God is made fully explicit either in some subordinate divine being called "Lord" or in some merely human figure uniquely appointed for this purpose and therefore designated "Son of God." But whatever their metaphysical differences, all such concepts and symbols perform essentially the same function in theistic religions. Just as "God" is used in these religions as the name for ultimate reality insofar as it is the *implicit* primal source of authentic self-understanding, so terms like "Word of God" or "Son of God" are used to designate some decisive re-presentation of God insofar as it is the *explicit* primal source of the same self-understanding.

And yet if this implies that all such terms are functionally interchangeable in that, despite their differences, they can all be used to identify the same decisive revelation of God, it is also true that even the same concepts and symbols can point to very different re-presentations of the meaning of God for us. In that event, it is some term such as "Son of God," say, that is used in one respect to *answer* the existential question, even while it can be used in another respect only to *ask* it, the material meaning of the term having become just what is in doubt.

It is at the level of theistic religious controversy represented by this quite specific doubt that the question addressed by all the New Testament christologies directly arises. Certainly if we are to judge from the honorific titles in terms of which they characteristically formulate the christological assertion, what is in question for them is just who really is Word of God, Son of God, Lord—in a word, the decisive re-presentation of God explicitly authorizing authentic existence. This is particularly striking in the case of the "I am" sayings in the Fourth Gospel, where, as we have seen, Jesus' "I" is really a predicate, not a subject, and the question he answers is not who he is, but what is to be designated by such terms as "the light of the world" and "the resurrection and the life." But, once again, this is in no way to suggest that the question presupposed by the christologies of the New Testament is anything other than the explicitly theistic question about God. For, as I have just explained, to ask about the identity of the decisive re-presentation of God is implicitly to ask about the identity of God, God being for theistic religions the implicit authorizing source of the same understanding of existence that is explicitly authorized by whatever decisively re-presents God.

On the other hand, because this question about God is properly religious rather than properly metaphysical, the question about the decisive re-presentation of God is in the last analysis simply a very specific way of asking the existential question about the meaning of ultimate reality for us. Consequently, what is finally at stake in any answer to it is indeed an answer to the question of God but only in the sense that it expresses an understanding at once of what alone is ultimately real and of what we ourselves are therefore given and called to be.

The conclusion at which we appear to have arrived, then, is this: contrary to the assumption typically made by revisionary and traditional christologies alike, the question christology answers is not simple but complex. It is not only a question about Jesus but also, and at one and the same time, a question about the meaning of ultimate reality for us. Thus it is what I call an *"existential-*historical" question, meaning thereby the kind of question that does indeed ask about what has actually happened, but that does so in such a way as to ask about its meaning for us here and now in the present rather than about its being in itself then and there in the past.

But this is to say that the question of christology as such, as it is in fact answered by the christological assertion, has a distinct logical structure. Specifically, it is distinct not only from the other kind of historical question that asks about the being of the past in itself, which I distinguish as *"empirical-historical,"* but also from what I have analyzed here as the existential question taken simply as such, independently of all particular historical experiences. It is important to be clear about this, because considering the main point I have tried to make, one might be led to suppose that the question christology answers simply is the existential question. This, however, it could not possibly be, because even though it is not *only* a question about Jesus, it very definitely *is* a question about Jesus; and this means that it could never so much as arise, much less ever be answered, except on the basis of particular historical experience of the Jesus about whose meaning for human existence it is the question.

Just what this means and does not mean for a correct understanding of the subject of the christological assertion we will need to inquire in the next chapter. The one thing that should already be clear is that both the subject of this assertion and any of its possible predicates must be the subject and the predicate of an assertion that can answer *this* christological question.

3. The Subject of the Christological Assertion

Our task in this first part of the book is not so much constructive as critical, in that we are concerned less with making the point of christology in the way in which a christology of reflection is called to make it than with talking about its point. To this end, I sought to show in the last chapter that and why the first point in the contemporary revisionary consensus is an untenable position. Contrary to the assumption that revisionary christologies typically continue to make, the question christology answers is not simply a question about Jesus, but also, and at the same time, a question about the meaning of ultimate reality for us. Thus it is what I called an "existential-historical" question, in that, while it most certainly asks about Jesus, the way in which it does so is determined by the fact that it asks even more fundamentally about the ultimate meaning of our own existence. As a consequence, it asks about the meaning of Jesus for us here and now in the present, not about the being of Jesus in himself then and there in the past.

If this argument is sound, however, we have already established the most fundamental thing to be said about the point of christology. Obviously the christological assertion that constitutes christology explicitly as such has to be an answer to the christological question. If, then, the christological question is an existential-historical question about the meaning of Jesus for us, the constitutive christological assertion has to be an answer to *this* existential-historical question. Specifically, it must be an assertion about Jesus that asserts his decisive significance for human existence by asserting that it is through him that the meaning of God for us, and hence the meaning of ultimate reality for us, is decisively re-presented. At the same time, the christological assertion must be an assertion about both ultimate reality and ourselves, in that it asserts conversely both that the ultimate reality that authorizes the authentic understanding of our existence is the God who is decisively revealed through Jesus and that the authentic self-understanding that is implicitly authorized by ultimate reality is the faith in God of which Jesus is the explicit authorizing source. If we keep in mind, then, that it is precisely the existential aspect of the christological question that is fundamental to its historical aspect, we may say, correspondingly, that it is precisely what the christological assertion asserts conversely about ultimate reality and ourselves that is fundamental to what it asserts about Jesus. In this sense, the point of christology is an existential point. Its assertion about who Jesus is is even more fundamentally an assertion about who we are—which is to say, of course, about who we are given and called to be by the mysterious ultimate reality determining our existence as human beings (Ogden, 1975b).

Because the point of the christological assertion is fundamentally existential, however, the question as to the subject of this assertion is absolutely crucial. If the answer to my existential question about what I myself am authorized to be by ultimate reality is the answer decisively re-presented through Jesus—and it is just this that the christological assertion fundamentally asserts—then obviously everything depends on determining just who Jesus is. It is precisely and only Jesus who gives what is otherwise a purely formal claim about his decisive significance for human existence and, conversely, about the meaning of ultimate reality for us its distinctive material meaning. But if this alone suffices to explain why we would need to pursue the question of this chapter in any adequate discussion of the point of christology, it is by no means the only reason that requires us to do so. On the contrary, at this point also, the prevailing consensus of revisionary christologies (although not *only* revisionary christologies) includes a position, in the form of an answer to this question, that I take to be so profoundly problematic as to be untenable. Consequently, if there is to be any solution to the problem of a revisionary christology such as we are seeking in this book, there is no way around so criticizing this prevailing answer as to argue for a very different understanding of the subject of the christological assertion.

Before proceeding with such a criticism, I should perhaps say a further word about just what the question is that we shall be trying to answer. Given what has already been said, it should be clear enough that, being the question about the subject of the christological assertion, it is concerned with determining the identity of Jesus. As such, however, it is concerned rather with *formally* identifying Jesus in a certain way than with determining his material identity—somewhat as one's concern in asking who Hamlet is in a given case might be satisfied by learning simply that he is a protagonist in a play by Shakespeare without learning anything more about his character as it is actually developed in this play. Just how Jesus needs to be formally identified in order to answer our question about him will become clear enough as the argument proceeds. The thing to keep in mind is the strictly formal character of both of the alternative answers that we shall be considering in this chapter. We shall not ask about the material identity of Jesus until Chapter 6, when we inquire about Jesus who is said to be Christ.

The first of the strictly formal answers, and the one that constitutes the second point in the revisionary consensus, is that the subject of the christological assertion is the so-called historical Jesus. In other words, the referent of the name "Jesus" in any such formulation of the christological assertion as "Jesus is the Christ" is the actual Jesus of the past insofar as he is knowable to us today by way of empirical-historical inquiry using the writings of the New Testament as sources. Thus, according to this answer, if this or any other formulation of the christological assertion is justified, it is so only because or insofar as certain empirical-historical claims about Jesus can somehow be established as true. It is for this reason that the revisionary christologies that answer our question in this way also typically insist on the historical possibility as well as the theological necessity of a quest of the historical Jesus. Because it is none other than the actual Jesus of history whom they take to be the subject of the christological assertion, they contend that neither the appropriateness nor the credibility of this assertion can possibly be established except by successfully conducting such a quest.

I have already indicated that I judge this answer to our question to be untenable, and I now want to give the reasons for this judgment. This I propose to do by reviewing the quest of the historical Jesus as it has developed from its origins in the theology of the Enlightenment to the so-called new quest of contemporary theology. Unless I am mistaken, to follow the main lines of this development is the best way to understand the profound problems that compel one to seek an alternative answer to the question.

The point has often been made that the motives behind the original quest of the historical Jesus were by no means merely historical. Far from being a disinterested inquiry about the past, it sprang from deep convictions that can be adequately described only as in their own way religious or theological (Ziolkowski, 1972: 40 f.). Thus, in seeking to penetrate behind the claims of traditional theology and dogma to Jesus as he really was, the original questers were guided by their assumption that the wholly human figure of Jesus himself, rather than either scripture or the tradition of the church, was the sole primary norm for judging the appropriateness of christological claims. This meant that such claims about Jesus could be justified as appropriate only insofar as he himself had explicitly advanced them. The longer the quest proceeded, however, the clearer it appeared that Jesus had not, in fact, made any claims for the decisive significance of his own person. Provided one oriented oneself to the synoptic gospels, which alone could be regarded as sources of reliable knowledge, one was compelled to conclude, in the words of a famous statement of Adolf von Harnack's, that "Not the Son, but only the Father, is included in the gospel as Jesus proclaimed it" (Harnack: 86). As such, of course, this was a historical rather than a theological conclusion. But as Harnack's own example fully confirmed, those who reached it typically took it to have the most direct theological consequences. Because of their underlying conviction that it is Jesus himself who is the real Christian canon, they immediately inferred from the fact that his gospel had included no christology that the same should be true of the church's gospel as well.

It was this properly theological inference that naturally proved to be the most challenging thing about the quest of the historical Jesus as it developed through the nineteenth century. In fact, more conservative Christians, who were oriented to the traditional christology based on scripture and dogma, stoutly resisted the claim of liberal theologians that it was "the religion *of* Jesus" rather than "the religion *about* Jesus" that is normative for the gospel of the church. Significantly, however, their resistance to this claim in no way questioned the guiding assumption of their liberal opponents that it is precisely the religion *of* Jesus that is the primary Christian norm. Quite the contrary, by arguing as they did that the religion *of* Jesus was itself already explicitly christological, and thus not really different from the religion *about* Jesus, they simply reinforced this underlying assumption. For them also the gospel of Jesus himself became in effect the real canon of the church. And so what was in reality a religious or theological difference about what is and is not appropriately Christian came to be discussed as though it were a historical difference about what Jesus had or had not in fact proclaimed. The result is that both parties to the dispute were to some extent self-deceived—the conservatives arguing for certain historical conclusions mainly because of their belief in the God-man of traditional christology, the liberals arguing against these same conclusions mainly because of their own belief in the merely human Jesus of critical history.

Such, in very general terms, was the situation that had emerged by the turn of the century. The quest of the historical Jesus that had begun as the project of a revisionary christology had come to be accepted even by defenders of traditional christology as not only historically possible but also theologically necessary. Events were soon to prove, however, that neither of these widely agreed upon assumptions was beyond question. As a matter of fact, it had already been questioned for some time whether it was really possible to write the life of Jesus as had originally been assumed, Harnack himself having habilitated in 1874 by defending the thesis, *Vita Jesu scribi nequit* (Zahn-Harnack: 46). Doubts about this were further confirmed, then, by the work of Martin Kähler, William Wrede, and Albert Schweitzer, which challenged any confidence that the course of Jesus' life and ministry could be reliably determined from the Gospel of Mark, which the two-source hypothesis for solving the synoptic problem had established as the earliest of the gospels.

The really serious challenge to the possibility of the quest came with the emergence of form criticism in the years immediately following World War I. If source criticism had already shown that the synoptic gospels are in effect collections of earlier traditions, one could still assume that at least the earliest of these traditions transmitted historical reports of what Jesus himself had said and done. But this assumption became ever harder to make with the work of form critics like Rudolf Bultmann, Martin Dibelius, and Karl Ludwig Schmidt. On their analyses, the primary interest of the early Christian community, to which we owe even the earliest of the traditions concerning Jesus, was religious rather than historical. Consequently, all the forms into which they proceeded to classify the individual traditions were forms of Christian kerygma—of bearing witness to Jesus as of decisive significance for the present, rather than reporting historically what he had said and done in the past. Simply in itself, naturally, this was a literary judgment about the forms of the earliest traditions, not a historical judgment about what could or could not be inferred from them were they to be used as historical sources (Ziolkowski, 1972: 30). But even if the form critics still allowed for the possibility of so using them—and, significantly, all three of the scholars referred to went on to write monographs on Jesus—the fact remains that anything like the original quest had now become quite impossible. Moreover, the kind of quest that was still allowed to be a possibility had been shown to involve a peculiar problem. Because all the sources about Jesus are at best secondary, and because even the earliest among them are witness rather than reportage, any control on what can be inferred from them about Jesus' own words and deeds first has to be reconstructed by inference from them.

It was Bultmann above all who appreciated the significance of this problem. In the introduction to his own monograph on Jesus, he delimited the only kind of quest that he took to be still possible to identifying "the complex of ideas" of which Jesus is represented as the bearer in the earliest stratum of the synoptic tradition. In doing so, however, he frankly admitted that "one naturally has no certainty that the words in this earliest stratum were actually spoken by Jesus. It could be that even its origin goes back to a complicated historical process that we are no longer able to trace" (Bult-

mann, 1951a: 15 f.). But if Bultmann thus raised the profoundest question about the historical possibility of a quest for
Jesus, he was also the theologian who more than any other
questioned its theological necessity.

To be sure, the dialectical theology projected by Karl
Barth had already broken with the liberal assumption that it
is the Jesus of history who is the real Christian canon. Without
reverting to the doctrine of scripture of Protestant orthodoxy, Barth had appealed to the Word of God of which
scripture is the primary witness as the explicit primal source
of all authority in the church. But if this had already implied
that a quest of the historical Jesus was far from theologically
necessary, it was in the kind of kerygmatic theology that
Bultmann, under Barth's influence, went on to develop that
this implication was most explicitly drawn. In fact, Bultmann
not only denied the necessity of a quest for Jesus, he even
questioned its legitimacy. It lies in the very nature of the
Christian kerygma, he argued, to confront its hearer with a
decision of faith. Consequently, if the hearer undertakes to
inquire back behind the kerygma in order somehow to justify
this decision, he or she is in effect evading it. Insofar, then,
as a quest for Jesus is motivated by any such attempt at
justification, Bultmann's contention was that it is so far from
being necessary as to be illegitimate (Bultmann, 1951b: 46;
1954: 106 f., 206 ff.).

It is just here, however, that there has proved to be more
than a little misunderstanding of Bultmann's intentions,
even by some who have imagined themselves to be following
him. Because in distinguishing the historical Jesus from the
Christ of the kerygma, Bultmann typically appealed to the
dominant New Testament proclamation of the cross and the
resurrection, he is widely supposed to have held that there
was no such thing as Christian faith prior to Easter and that,
except for the crucifixion, the life and ministry of Jesus were

without any decisive significance. In fact, however, Bultmann held neither of these positions. He was emphatic in arguing that the Easter faith of the disciples was their way of remaking the same decision that they had already made by following Jesus during his lifetime and that the cross came to have the kind of meaning it had for them because it raised once again the same question that had already been raised by Jesus' proclamation (Bultmann, 1951b: 43; 1965: 47). The reason for drawing attention to this is to correct the widespread impression that, in appealing to the Christ of the kerygma against the historical Jesus, Bultmann intended to take up a position that is the extreme contrary to revisionary christology. The truth of the matter is that the position he assumed and defended was so far from simply abandoning the project of revisionary christology as to open up the possibility of a new and more adequate way of realizing its aims.

Even so, it was not this possibility that was to be realized during the ensuing phase of christological reflection. On the contrary, there was a shift away from Bultmann's position in the direction of insisting once again on the theological necessity of a quest for Jesus; and the remarkable thing is that this shift was initiated from within the circle of Bultmann's own most prominent students. Beginning with a famous lecture by Ernst Käsemann in 1953, there developed what James M. Robinson subsequently described as "a new quest of the historical Jesus" (Käsemann, 1954; J. M. Robinson). Although proponents of the new quest professed to accept the methods and results of form criticism, most of them tended to ignore the profound question that had been raised by Bultmann and to express considerable confidence about what could be known about the actual Jesus by controlled inference from the earliest layer of Jesus-traditions. In this connection, many of them increasingly gave attention to developing "criteria of authenticity" whereby one could determine what in even these earliest traditions could or could not be attributed to Jesus himself (Fuller, 1966: 94–98; Perrin: 38–47).

But if the new questers thus tried to show that a quest for Jesus was after all historically possible, the most striking thing about their project was the conviction underlying it that it was in any event theologically necessary. Just as the old quest was at bottom religious or theological in arguing for the discontinuity between Jesus as he really was and the picture of him in scripture and dogma, so the new quest was similarly motivated in arguing instead for their continuity. Käsemann for one was quite frank about this, especially when, in looking back some twenty years later, he defended the thesis that "if there is really anything new about the 'new quest,' it lies decisively in the realm of the dogmatic interests motivating it and their more precise characterization" (Käsemann, 1975: 52). But the same motivation had already become clear enough from the typical assumption of the new questers that no christological formulation can be justified as appropriate that cannot claim support in the historical Jesus. As Gerhard Ebeling put the point, "If Jesus had never lived, or if faith in him were shown to be a misunderstanding of the significance of the historical Jesus, then, clearly, the ground would be taken out from under Christian faith. If it lost its support in the historical Jesus, it would perhaps not be devoid of an object altogether, but it would be devoid of the object that the Christian proclamation has continually put forth as the central object of faith" (Ebeling: 51).

Generally speaking, one may say that it is this position represented by the new quest that is now taken, in one form or another, by virtually all revisionary christologies. Indeed, as I have indicated, essentially the same position is assumed even by defenders of traditional christology, who are concerned with reformulating rather than with replacing it. Nevertheless, it should already be apparent from the preceding review that this position is by no means without difficulties. Provided one still takes seriously the methods and results of form criticism, it is so profoundly problematic that one simply cannot any longer maintain it. This becomes particularly clear, I believe, in the case of a theologian who, unlike most of the other new questers, has been unwilling to ignore what he calls "the form-critical reservation" about using the earliest traditions concerning Jesus as historical sources.

The theologian to whom I refer is the New Testament scholar Willi Marxsen. I first became convinced of the significance of his work when I encountered his unconventional treatment of the question of the canon and his independent development of the notion that the so-called Christ-kerygma, which Bultmann had typically taken to be the real norm of christology, is not the only kerygma of which the New Testament writings provide evidence (Marxsen, 1969). Marxsen's insistence that there is also what he calls "the Jesus-kerygma," represented by the earliest stratum of the synoptic tradition, I found liberating in that it seemed to allow one to get beyond the impasse represented by the other, more conventional alternatives: either "the so-called historical Jesus" or else "the historic, biblical Christ" (in Kähler's terms), or "the Christ of the kerygma" (in the words of Bultmann). If Marxsen was right, one could agree with Kähler and Bultmann that the norm of christology is indeed provided by the witness to Christ in the Bible or in the kerygma, rather than by the historical Jesus, even while maintaining more clearly than either of them had done that it is not the Christ-kerygma of Paul and John that constitutes this norm, but rather the Jesus-kerygma accessible through critical analysis of the synoptic gospels. To this extent at least something in the quest of the historical Jesus, old and new, could also be preserved and re-expressed.

The more I have studied Marxsen, however, the clearer it

has become to me that his position is a more nuanced, subtle, or—as I have finally come to believe—confused position than I first supposed. Although he tends to side closely with Bultmann in his assessment of the New Testament writings as historical sources—arguing that they are all documents expressing the witness of faith rather than historical reports—he at the same time tends to side, rather, with Bultmann's leading students in insisting that a new quest of the historical Jesus is theologically necessary. Marxsen also agrees with Bultmann, to be sure, that no such quest could even conceivably suffice to justify the truth of the constitutive christological assertion. Being a matter of faith, this assertion could not possibly be established as true simply by empirical-historical inquiry, and any supposition to the contrary plays into the hands of those who wish to avoid the unavoidable risk of faith. But like Käsemann, Ebeling, and others, Marxsen distinguishes between using empirical-historical inquiry illegitimately to justify the *truth* of the kerygma and using such inquiry legitimately to establish the *authority* of the kerygma as appropriately Christian. According to the kerygma itself, Jesus is the source of its authority, in that, as Marxsen puts it, "in bearing their witness of faith, the witnesses mean, rightly or wrongly, to speak of Jesus." Therefore, as much as one may agree with Bultmann that there can be no historical inquiry back behind the kerygma in order to justify the truth of its christological claim, one must agree at the same time with Bultmann's students and critics that there has to be a historical inquiry behind the kerygma in order to justify it as Christian kerygma. To this extent, Marxsen expressly affirms his agreement with the statement of Ebeling cited earlier, that no christological formulation can be theologically justified that cannot claim support in the historical Jesus (1969: 112, 149, 257).

Consistent with his agreement with this position, Marxsen time and again discusses how theologically impossible our

situation would be if empirical-historical inquiry were to establish that the actual Jesus of history did not himself assert
or imply the claim that the kerygma makes or implies concerning him. In that event, he reasons, one would have to
either surrender the Christian kerygma as an error or else,
believing the kerygma to be true, make it "the real locus of
revelation," contrary to its own intention in pointing to Jesus
as this locus. In this connection, Marxsen sometimes speaks,
very much as Käsemann typically does, of the implicit doce-
tism of locating revelation in the kerygma rather than in
Jesus himself (160 ff., 112, 248; Käsemann, 1975: 50, 52, 57).

Consequently, for all of his acceptance of the methods and
results of form criticism and its reservation concerning the
use of our sources, Marxsen insists on the theological necessity of a new quest to justify the claims of any constructive
christology. And yet just because he really does take form
criticism seriously—rather more so, in my opinion, than either Käsemann or Ebeling—he again and again forces the
question whether the new quest for whose theological necessity he argues is after all a historical possibility; and, again,
unlike so many others who hold essentially the same position,
he does not allow himself to be reassured by the fallacious
inference that the quest must somehow be possible historically simply because it is necessary theologically. Quite the
contrary, he frankly admits that "the so-called historical Jesus
cannot be immediately reached," because the last point to
which empirical-historical inquiry can take us is not the actual Jesus himself, but rather just that Jesus-kerygma, or earliest witness to Jesus, that is the most we can reconstruct from
the synoptic gospels. Strictly speaking, all we can ever hope
to talk about is not what Jesus said and did, but what Jesus was
heard to have said and *seen* to have done by those on whose
experience and memory of him we are utterly dependent.
On the basis of this frank admission, then, Marxsen allows
that what is historical in the earliest Jesus-traditions is "not

an isolated Jesus, whom one could assert to be the ground of faith independently of one's own faith," but rather "the testimonies to Jesus as the ground of faith by the earliest witnesses." It is in these earliest testimonies, this Jesus-kerygma, that christological formulations must be able to claim support if they are to be justified as appropriate (261, 152, 262).

But now, clearly, it is one thing to be able to claim support in *Jesus himself,* something else again to be able to claim support only in *the earliest testimonies to Jesus.* If the second is sufficient to justify christological formulations, the first is unnecessary; if, on the contrary, the first is necessary, the second is insufficient. This, then, is the dilemma of Marxsen's position, which he never succeeds in overcoming, even if there are indications in his writings that he might well be open to the alternative answer to our question that I shall presently be urging (1976b: 141 ff.). Even so, the reason Marxsen is of more help than anyone else in understanding the problems of the first answer is that he has not been willing to evade these problems by reassurances about the possibility of the quest for Jesus that have no basis in the nature of our sources.

This is to imply that nothing in either the methods or the results of the new quest warrants an assessment of our sources other than that already reached by Bultmann and confirmed by Marxsen. Despite all the efforts that have been made to develop criteria of authenticity, the fact remains that our only sources for Jesus are at best secondary and, in their controlling concern, witnesses of faith, not historical reports. Thus, as Marxsen effectively shows, the traditions redacted in the gospels can be compared to a historical drama. In the one case just as in the other the controlling concern is not to provide information about the past, but rather so to make use of historical material as to say something significant to the present. In the case of many a historical drama, however, we have independent sources of information by comparison with which we can determine how much in it is authentically historical. But in the case of the gospel traditions, Marxsen argues, "we are not in this fortunate position, for we can only compare one kerygma with another, never kerygma with historical material" (1969: 258 f.).

Consequently, even the "criterion of dissimilarity" (or of "dual irreducibility"), which Norman Perrin frankly confesses to be "the one sure criterion," cannot be made to yield authentic Jesus-material without begging the question (Perrin: 45; cf. 38). This is so at any rate unless one admits from the outset that the only evidence one can ever have for anything that Jesus is inferred to have said or done is what he is represented as having said or done by those to whom we owe the earliest Christian witness now accessible to us. But to admit this is to allow that, by the very nature of our sources, there can never be any distinction with respect to evidence, and in this sense any operational distinction, between Jesus as he actually was and Jesus as he is represented in the earliest stratum of witness that can now be reconstructed from the synoptic gospels. At this absolutely fundamental point, "post-Bultmannian" theology has left everything exactly where it found it; and it is the great strength of Marxsen's work to have clearly recognized this instead of trying somehow to ignore or evade it.

But if the dilemma of Marxsen's position makes clear why the first answer to our question is indeed untenable, I should not want to give the impression that a quest of the historical Jesus is theologically unnecessary only because it is now seen to be historically impossible. To reason so would evidently be no less fallacious than to suppose, as so many seem to do, that the theological necessity of such a quest in some way justifies their confidence in its historical possibility. My position, however, is that a quest for Jesus is and would be theologically unnecessary, regardless of any question whether it is also historically possible. This is so, I maintain, because the real subject of the christological assertion is not the historical Jesus, or, as we may now say more precisely, the *empirical-*historical Jesus, for which the earliest stratum of Christian witness must be used as historical source. Rather, the subject of the christological assertion is correctly identified formally as the *existential-*historical Jesus, for which this same earliest stratum of Christian witness plays the very different role of theological norm.

This, of course, is the alternative answer to our question that was already given implicitly in the analysis of the christological question in the preceding chapter. But if it is correct, as I now wish to urge it is, what our sources do or do not permit in the way of inferences concerning the empirical-historical Jesus is simply of no theological consequence.

That this must be so becomes clear, I think, as soon as one understands the distinction I have now made explicit between the empirical-historical Jesus and the existential-historical Jesus. To illumine this distinction, I wish to make use of it in an analogy suggested by H. Richard Niebuhr's now classic discussion in *The Meaning of Revelation* of the difference between "internal" and "external" history. Niebuhr illustrates this important difference by contrasting the obvious reference to the event of 4 July 1776 in the opening sentence of Lincoln's Gettysburg Address with the description given of the same event in the *Cambridge Modern History* (Niebuhr, 1941: 60 ff.). The significance of this illustration for our discussion lies in its forceful clarification of what an American patriot such as Lincoln means in speaking of the event that was the origin of his nation. Clearly, he means nothing other or less than an actual happening, prior to and distinct from both his own patriotic devotion and that of all other American patriots who have preceded him, right back to the founding fathers. And yet it is just as clear that the only event the patriot thus means to refer to is the existential-historical event that, in originating the American nation, is the primal authorizing source of his own and all other appropriately American patriotism. This is why the whole meaning of the event as Lincoln refers to it is summed up by identifying it simply as the bringing forth of "a new nation, conceived in liberty, and dedicated to the proposition that all men are created equal." Whatever else may in fact have happened, as empirical-historical research might be able to establish, the only thing about the event that is of interest to Lincoln or to other American patriots as such is that it is the origin of a nation so conceived and so dedicated, and hence the primal authorizing source of their own as well as all other authentic Americanism.

Analogously, I should say, the event that the New Testament witnesses as such mean in referring to Jesus does indeed belong to the origin of the Christian church, and so is an actual happening, prior to and independent of not only their own faith and witness, but even the original faith and witness of the apostles in which everything Christian originates. But there is the further analogy that in this case too the whole meaning of the event, so far as the New Testament is concerned, is expressed by formulations that, in one conceptuality and symbolism or another, represent it as the existential-historical event that is at once the decisive revelation of God and the primal authorizing source of all that is appropriately Christian. Thus the referent of the name "Jesus" in any such formulation as "Jesus is the Christ" is not someone whom we first come to know more or less probably only by empirical-historical inquiry back behind the witness of the apostles as well as the witnesses of the New Testament. Rather, "Jesus" refers to the one whom we already know most certainly through the same apostolic witness as well as all other witnesses of faith insofar as they are conformed to the witness of the apostles.

This means then that, while Marxsen is quite right that the

New Testament witnesses mean, rightly or wrongly, to speak of Jesus in bearing their witness, he is misled in assuming that the Jesus of whom they mean to speak can only be the empirical-historical Jesus. To be sure, the earliest witnesses, to whom we owe what Marxsen calls the Jesus-kerygma, apparently make any number of assumptions about Jesus that are empirical-historical in character. They not only seem to assume that Jesus proclaimed or taught certain things or acted in certain ways, but also that he had a certain understanding of himself and his ministry that led him to confront his hearers with an extraordinary claim. But the question, of course, is what in all of this really does have the character of an empirical-historical assumption about Jesus, as distinct from being a certain way of bearing witness to his decisive significance. Assuming, as we must, that even this earliest stratum of Jesus-tradition is witness of faith and not historical reportage, we have to allow for the possibility that even what clearly seem to be assumptions about Jesus as he actually was are really assertions about Jesus as he truly is—which is to say, as he is *believed to be* by those who by means of such assertions intend to bear witness to him as the decisive re-presentation of God.

One thinks, for example, of the sayings in the earliest stratum of the synoptic tradition where Jesus is represented as so speaking of the imminent reign of God and of the coming of the Son of Man as to imply an extraordinary claim for the significance of himself and his words (Luke 12:8 f.; Mark 8:38). What is certain from these sayings is not that those to whom we owe them assumed that Jesus actually spoke in this way, however probable it may be that they in fact did so, but rather that what they meant by Jesus in so representing him was the one through whom both they themselves and the hearers of their own witness were decisively confronted with just such a claim.

This is not to suggest, naturally, that all of the claims that are made or implied about Jesus in the earliest tradition were intended as assertions of faith. However difficult it may be to identify particular claims that were intended as empirical-historical, there seems to be no reason to doubt that many of them certainly were so intended; and to this extent, Marxsen might well appear to be correct in assuming that it is of the empirical-historical Jesus that the earliest witnesses mean to speak. But here we must be careful to avoid a possible confusion. What the witnesses *assert* about Jesus in speaking of him as the subject of their christological formulations is one thing; what they *assume* about Jesus in so speaking of him is something else. I see no reason to deny that many of the claims that are made or implied about Jesus in the earliest witness were understood by those who made them as empirical-historical claims. In representing Jesus as saying this or doing that, they quite clearly assumed, rightly or wrongly, that he had in fact so spoken or acted. But the thing to note is that they assumed this, they did not assert it—not at any rate in making or implying the constitutive christological assertion. So far as *this* assertion is concerned, all the claims they made or implied were not about what *Jesus* had said and done, but rather about what *God* had said and done and was still saying and doing precisely through Jesus, and thence through their own witness of faith. In other words, whatever their assumptions about the being of Jesus in himself as a figure of the past, their assertions all had to do with the meaning of Jesus for us as he still confronts us in the present. They were all assertions about Jesus as the decisive re-presentation of God and, therefore, as the one through whom the meaning of ultimate reality and the authentic understanding of our own existence are made fully explicit. Because this is so, I contend that the Jesus to whom the earliest witnesses point as "the real locus of revelation" is the existential-historical Jesus, and therefore neither the empirical-historical Jesus nor their own witness of faith, save insofar as it is solely through their witness that this event of revelation is now accessible and continues to take place.

If this contention is correct, however, what can or cannot be inferred concerning the empirical-historical Jesus has no bearing whatever on the point of christology. Whether Jesus did or did not teach any explicit christology, the claim made about him by the constitutive christological assertion may still be entirely appropriate. Of course, this much of what I am saying has long since come to be accepted by a large number of theologians. Contrary to the shared assumption of liberals and conservatives earlier on, that christology can be included in the gospel of the church only if it was explicitly included in the gospel of Jesus, many theologians now recognize that there is another option between the liberal and conservative extremes. Provided that Jesus at least implied a claim for the decisive significance of himself and his work, whether he also taught an explicit christology may well be regarded as a merely historical question without any theological significance one way or the other. But as different as this kind of a position indeed is from both of the older alternatives, liberal and conservative alike, it still completely agrees with them in the underlying assumption that christological formulations can be justified as appropriate only insofar as at least some empirical-historical claims about Jesus can be shown to be true. Thus even theological moderates who hold that Jesus taught no more than an "implicit christology" still typically insist on the theological necessity of a quest of the historical Jesus to establish at least this (Brown, 1975: 20–37).

If I am right, however, the appropriateness of the christological assertion is as little dependent on showing that Jesus made at least an implicit christological claim as on showing that he taught an explicit christology. Because the subject of the christological assertion is Jesus in his meaning for us, not Jesus in his being in himself, whether he did or did not imply a claim for the decisive significance of his own person has no bearing whatever on the appropriateness of this assertion. Whether he implied any such claim or not, the fact remains that what those to whom we owe even the earliest Christian witness mean in so speaking of him is the one through whom they themselves have been confronted with such a claim and who still continues to make it through their own witness of faith.

To this extent, the alternative answer to our question for which I am arguing implies that the claims that are made or implied about Jesus from the earliest witnesses on are not subject to any empirical-historical control. But if this implication is not to be misunderstood, two things need to be clearly kept in mind.

For one thing, I am in no way implying that all the claims that Christians make or imply about Jesus are beyond the control of empirical-historical inquiry. Quite the contrary, I have already insisted on clearly distinguishing between what the earliest witnesses *assert* about Jesus as the subject of their christological formulations and what they may very well *assume* about him in doing so. If the first of these is indeed beyond even the possibility of empirical-historical control—and this is my contention—this certainly is not the case with the second. In fact, I should insist that no empirical-historical assumption about Jesus whatever could be exempt from such control. Even the assumption that the primal source that is most certainly known as explicitly authorizing Christian existence was an individual person whose proper name was "Jesus" can be established as true only by empirical-historical inquiry. And the same must be said for any assumptions that this person had a certain understanding of himself and his vocation, that he preached and taught certain things and performed certain acts, and that he ran afoul of religious and political authorities and was tried, condemned, and executed. All such assumptions are clearly subject to empirical-historical inquiry, and none of them can be either known to be true or shown to be false except by means of such inquiry (Nineham, 1977: 76–91).

The other thing that must be kept in mind is more important: I have no intention of questioning, much less denying, either that all christological formulations must be justified as appropriate or that the only way to justify them is by empirical-historical inquiry. Nothing is more obvious, even in the writings collected in the New Testament, than the variety of formulations whereby the constitutive christological assertion has been expressed or implied. Moreover, if one avoids an unhistorical harmonization of these various formulations, one can hardly fail to observe that many of them are sufficiently different in certain respects as to be mutually exclusive. Consequently, since all of these formulations purport to express one and the same witness of faith, it is necessary to inquire of each of them whether it appropriately does so. But if this makes clear why christological formulations simply have to be justified, it is equally obvious that there is no way to justify them except by testing their claim to express one and the same Christian witness. And this can be done only by inquiring back behind each formulation to the normative witness of faith that it claims to formulate. My position, however, is that this clearly necessary process of empirical-historical inquiry ultimately becomes not a quest of the historical Jesus, but rather a quest of the earliest Christian witness. Because the subject of the christological assertion is not Jesus in his being in himself, but rather Jesus in his meaning for us, it is precisely this earliest Christian witness, in which the decisive significance of Jesus is first expressed, that is the normative witness of faith by which the appropriateness of all christological formulations must be justified.

Thus, in my position no less than in the alternative position of revisionary christology, empirical-historical inquiry is very definitely a theological necessity. Furthermore, I entirely agree that the critical step in such inquiry is so to analyze the writings of the New Testament as to reconstruct the earliest stratum of the tradition of witness lying behind them. But where the position I have defended clearly does differ from the alternative, and differs from it not merely circumstantially but in principle, is in understanding the final objective of such inquiry and the proper role therein of this earliest stratum of witness. Far from understanding this earliest witness as at best the historical source from which the norm for christological claims still has to be inferred, I have contended that this stratum of witness is itself the norm of appropriateness and that the Jesus to whom it bears witness is, accordingly, the real subject of the christological assertion.

4. The Conditions of Asserting a Christological Predicate

The preceding chapters have all been concerned with "the problem of a revisionary christology." Having tried to clarify this problem in general terms in the first chapter, I have attempted in the two chapters that followed to consider further two specific questions, answers to which go to make up a consensus among contemporary revisionary christologies. In each of these chapters, my argument has been directed toward showing, first, that the answer to the question that is given in this revisionary consensus is untenable, and, second, that another, more adequate answer to the question can and should be given. Insofar as this argument has succeeded, we have already taken two important steps toward solving our problem by learning to talk more adequately about the point of christology.

First, and most important, we have learned that the question christology answers is not simple but complex, that it is not only a question about Jesus but also and more fundamentally a question about the ultimate meaning of our own existence. Following from this we have learned, second, that the subject of the christological assertion cannot be the empirical-historical Jesus, whom we first come to know only more or less probably by way of inference from the earliest stratum of Christian witness. On the contrary, the Jesus who is said to be Christ can only be the existential-historical Jesus, whom we already know most certainly through any Christian witness whatever insofar as it is conformed to this same earliest witness as its primary norm. In sum: because the question of christology is fundamentally existential, the same must be said of the assertion that answers it; and this means that the subject of the assertion is not Jesus in his being in himself as he once lived in the past, but rather Jesus in his meaning for us as he still lives in the present through the Christian witness of faith.

Our concern in this chapter is to continue this same line of critical argument by considering further yet a third point in the revisionary consensus. This is the point that has to do with the predicate of the christological assertion and, more exactly, with the conditions that must be satisfied in order to truthfully assert any such predicate. According to the position typically taken by revisionary christologies, Jesus can be truthfully said to be Christ, or any of the other things that the christology of witness has appropriately asserted or implied him to be, if, but only if, he himself, as a human person, perfectly actualized the possibility of authentic self-understanding. Thus the sufficient as well as the necessary conditions of truthful predication implied by any appropriate christological predicate lie in the being of Jesus in himself, in his own personal relation to the ultimate reality called "God" and, specifically, in his having unfailingly understood himself in the way authorized by this ultimate reality. Of course, there are any number of concepts and symbols in which revisionary christologies have formulated this position, from speaking about the absolute constancy of Jesus' God-consciousness or his unbroken realization of eternal God-manhood to speaking about the perfection of his faith and obedience or his utter responsiveness to the self-expressive activity of God. But however different they may be in their particular concepts and symbols, revisionary christologies are typically the same in their essential claim: Jesus is what the christological assertion asserts him to be because, but only because, he is the one human being who consistently understood his own existence in the authentic way in which all human beings are given and called to do.

The other thing to observe about this claim is that it is the one really distinctive claim of revisionary christology. In its understanding of the question of christology and, to a considerable extent, even in its understanding of the subject of the christological assertion, revisionary christology is hardly different from the traditional christology it is intended to replace or at least to reformulate. But where it undoubtedly is different and truly revisionary is in holding that the necessary and sufficient conditions of truthfully making the christological assertion are to be found in Jesus' unique understanding of his existence in relation to God. This difference is particularly striking in the case of revisionary christologies that frankly understand themselves as thereby replacing the traditional doctrine of the incarnation (Faut: 64–102). But even in the case of revisionary christologies that think of themselves as thereby reformulating this doctrine rather than as replacing it, there is still the difference between their own "christology from below" and the traditional "christology from above." Their contention, indeed, is that by thus beginning from below and grounding the christological assertion in Jesus' unique self-understanding, they not only at last do justice to the traditional claim that he is truly man, but they also ground their christological formulations in just that experience of Jesus by the earliest community of which the traditional doctrine of the incarnation is itself an expression (Rahner, 1972: 227–238; 1975: 353–369; Rahner and Weger: 197 f.).

Unless I am mistaken, however, this third point in the revisionary consensus is no less problematic than the other two. One of my reasons for thinking this will already be apparent from the preceding discussion. If it is impossible to justify the appropriateness of christological formulations by showing support for them in the historical Jesus, one obviously cannot justify their credibility if it requires showing the same kind of support. But this is not the only reason for thinking that the typical revisionary understanding of the truth conditions of the christological assertion is also untenable. In fact, as I now propose to show, it is open to other objections, theological as well as historical, that are considerably more serious.

First of all, however, I want to say a further word about the one objection that is already apparent from what was said in the last chapter. My argument there, it will be recalled, is that it lies in the very nature of our sources that there can never be any operational distinction between Jesus as he really was and Jesus as he is represented in the earliest of these sources. Because the only evidence we have for the first is strictly identical with such evidence as we have for the second, any distinction we make between them must either remain merely theoretical or else beg the question. If this means that we can never hope to talk about what Jesus said and did, as distinct from what he was heard to have said and seen to have done by those whose witness to him provides our earliest sources, it just as surely means that we can never hope to talk about Jesus' own self-understanding, as distinct from how he was understood to have understood himself by these same earliest witnesses. Of course, one might conceivably attempt to infer Jesus' self-understanding indirectly from material authentically reporting his sayings and actions. But aside from the fact that, as I shall presently show, the warrants for any such inference cannot be sufficiently backed up to be acceptable, there remains the peculiar problem of distinguishing between Jesus' own sayings and actions and the words and deeds attributed to him in the earliest Christian witness. I conclude, therefore, that if Jesus can be truthfully said to be Christ, or any of the other things that Christians have appropriately asserted or implied him to be, only insofar as he had an authentic understanding of his own existence, then, whether this can be truthfully said or not must in the nature of the case remain an unanswered question.

This conclusion is unavoidable, however, even if one assumes a very different assessment of our sources from the one for which I have argued. This is so at any rate as soon as one clears up certain ambiguities that commonly attend the discussion of our question by revisionary christologies.

As I have indicated, one of the ways in which such christologies formulate their essential claim is by speaking of the perfection of Jesus' faith. It is well known, however, that the word "faith" is systematically ambiguous insofar as it can refer either to the objective beliefs believed in *(fides quae creditur)* or to the subjective act of believing *(fides qua creditur)*. To speak, then, as revisionary theologians commonly do, of "the faith of Jesus" is insofar ambiguous until one specifies whether what is intended by such speaking is the objective faith *in which* Jesus believed or rather the subjective faith *by which* he believed. The reason this ambiguity is important is that as a general rule the objective faith of a person can be more readily determined from what he or she says or does than his or her subjective faith. However confident one may be in inferring from a person's particular words and deeds to his or her objective beliefs, one can hardly be anything like as confident in inferring from the same data to the consistency or sincerity of the person's subjective believing.

Nor is this the only important ambiguity in speaking of faith generally and of the faith of Jesus in particular. Certainly in the theological tradition shaped by the insights of the Reformation, there are reasons for distinguishing between a broad and a strict sense of the term "faith," understood as meaning subjective believing. Taken strictly, the term refers to the innermost act of the person whereby he or she trusts in the gift of God's love and on the basis of such trust is also loyal to the demand of the same love. But "faith" may also be taken broadly insofar as the loyalty that is the active moment of thus responding to God's love—trust being its passive moment—inevitably works through love and thence through good works. Because the good works through which faith thus finds expression are the works of faith itself, faith may be understood broadly, as including its good works, rather than strictly, in distinction from them. But if faith *lato sensu* is something outward and visible insofar as the works of faith can indeed be seen and judged by human beings, faith *stricto sensu* is something inward and invisible that God alone can see and judge. Once again, then, it is important to be clear about the sense of "faith" when one speaks of the faith of Jesus. If what is meant in so speaking is Jesus' faith in the broad sense of the word, it was at least in principle experienceable by those who knew him and hence was a possible topic of empirical-historical judgment. But if what is meant is rather Jesus' faith in the strict sense of that innermost trust and loyalty that alone is saving faith, there is as little reason to suppose that anyone could experience and make empirical-historical judgments about Jesus' faith as about the faith of any other human person.

It is with these ambiguities in mind that I have ventured to formulate the position of revisionary christology by speaking not of Jesus' faith but of his self-understanding and, specifically, of his having perfectly actualized the possibility of authentic self-understanding authorized by ultimate reality. To be sure, the term "self-understanding" also could conceivably be used objectively as well as subjectively and broadly as well as strictly, in which case it would be just as ambiguous as the word "faith." But in the sense in which I have consistently used the term throughout this discussion, it refers exclusively to the subjective act of understanding one's own existence as a human person, which I have expressly distinguished from the necessary implications of such an act, moral as well as metaphysical. Thus, when I speak of revisionary christologies' typically locating the necessary and sufficient conditions of truthfully asserting a christological predicate in Jesus' having perfectly actualized the possibility of authentic self-understanding, I intend to clear up both of the ambiguities to which I have drawn attention. I intend to remove any doubt that it is of the innermost act of Jesus' own subjectivity that revisionary christologies presume to speak in specifying the truth conditions of the christological assertion.

Once such doubts are removed, however, the conclusion is inescapable that one cannot possibly answer the question whether the conditions necessary for making this assertion are in fact satisfied. Even if one assumes that authentic Jesus-material can somehow be distinguished from the witness of the earliest church, the fact remains that the faith of Jesus in the strict sense of the word is not and, in the nature of the case, could not be an empirical-historical datum. At best it has to be inferred from what are taken to be authentic reports of his sayings and actions; and attending this inference, exactly like any other inference of the same kind, are the difficulties already mentioned—of inferring anything with confidence about a person's subjective believing much less about his or her innermost act of self-understanding. Moreover, there are two other difficulties in this case that are evidently insuperable. On the one hand, if what is to be inferred is that Jesus' self-understanding was consistently authentic, in that throughout his entire life he unfailingly understood himself as a human being is given and called to do, the data base that is required to make such an inference so much as plausible indefinitely exceeds what could be reasonably claimed in the case of any human being, even one about whom we may claim to know indefinitely more than we can conceivably claim in the case of Jesus. On the other hand, if the conclusion of scholars for the last hundred years is sound, that no one can possibly write a life of Jesus, because our earliest sources concerning him provide insufficient evidence of his inner and outer development, how can anyone possibly infer from the same sources that there was no point in his entire life when his self-understanding was anything but authentic (Harvey and Ogden: 82–87; Hick [ed.]: 186–195)?

One way of trying to respond to this question is by invoking warrants that rule out any alternative inference. Thus James P. Mackey, for example, asserts in his recent book, *Jesus, the Man and the Myth,* that "there is really no possibility of dissimulation" in such cases, because "power-seeking in service, like condescension in giving, or cowardly envy in forgiving, is too easily perceptible, if sometimes, unfortunately perceived too late, and no good comes of it, no sense of life and existence as grace, no faith or love, no hope." Invoking this as a warrant, Mackey infers from "the public ministry of Jesus" on behalf of the imminent reign of God to what he carefully distinguishes as "the personal faith of Jesus himself (the faith which was a quality of Jesus as personal subject, not the faith of which Jesus is object)." In this way, he concludes that "Jesus cherished all life and existence, and especially other people, as God's precious gift, and so, without ulterior motive, he accepted all and served their needs, and so enabled and inspired them to discover the treasure hidden in their lives" (Mackey: 170 f., 161, 163). But how sound is the warrant that licenses this conclusion? Is the backing that Mackey gives for it sufficient to make it acceptable?

Surely there is as much to be said for the precisely contrary claim of Søren Kierkegaard, when he insists on interpreting his statement that certain persons "have believed" as meaning that they "have said that they believed." This he does on the ground that "no man can control the profession of another further than this; even if the other has endured, borne, suffered all for the faith, an outsider cannot get beyond what he says about himself, for a lie can be stretched precisely as far as the truth—in the eyes of men, but not in the sight of God" (Kierkegaard: 86). As a matter of fact, if I must choose between Kierkegaard's claim that a lie can be stretched precisely as far as the truth and Mackey's claim that there is really no possibility of dissimulation, the first seems to me by far the stronger warrant. This is particularly true when I keep in mind that what is at issue is inferring the presence of faith in the strict sense of the word. Provided faith is understood as the innermost act of trust in God's love and loyalty to it, one must say of any of its putative expressions what Paul says of even the highest expressions of love: even "if I give away all I have, and if I deliver my body to be burned," the possibility remains that I "have not love" (1 Cor. 13:3).

Because this is so, it is not possible even in principle to infer Jesus' authentic self-understanding from empirical-historical evidence concerning his words and deeds. Granted that anyone who understood himself authentically would say and do what Jesus is represented as having said and done, the converse claim still may not hold and, therefore, can never license an inference concerning the authenticity of his self-understanding.

For all the usual revisionary christology could even possibly show, then, the christological assertion must remain groundless, the conditions for truthfully asserting it being such that in principle as well as in fact they could never be known to be satisfied. Theoretically, of course, one might try to meet this objection by frankly arguing that, since Jesus is a unique case, claims about his self-understanding need not conform to the requirements of such claims in the case of all other human beings. But any such argument would seem to imply simply one more qualification of the true humanity of Jesus and, therefore, could hardly commend itself to a revisionary christology that hopes at last to avoid all such qualifications. On the other hand, given the essential claim of such a christology as to the conditions of christological predication, the price of consistently affirming that Jesus is truly man is painfully high. This is especially clear in the case of revisionary christologies that seek to reformulate the traditional doctrine of the incarnation instead of frankly replacing it. Far from grounding their christological formulations in the very experience of Jesus by the earliest community of which this traditional doctrine is said to be the expression, they succeed in showing only that its "christology from above" is and must be as experientially groundless as their own "christology from below."

This leads directly to the further objection that this understanding of the conditions of christological predication can claim no support whatever in the christologies of witness characteristic of the New Testament. Despite attempts that are repeatedly made to evade or overthrow it, Rudolf Bultmann's statement still stands, that "neither do the gospels speak of Jesus' own faith nor does the kerygma make any reference to Jesus' faith" (Bultmann, 1967: 461). But if Bultmann is right about this, there is no question that the writers of the New Testament could hardly have reasoned in the manner of the usual revisionary christology. For if they had supposed for a moment that the faith of Jesus was the sufficient or even a necessary condition of his being who they asserted or implied him to be, they obviously could not have failed so completely to make any reference to it.

But even if Bultmann's statement should prove to need qualification—because it can be shown, for example, that the gospels at least *imply* certain claims about Jesus' faith—the conclusion to be drawn therefrom about the truth conditions of the christological assertion certainly need not be that typical of revisionary christology. If it is true of our sources, as I argued in the last chapter, that what appear to be empirical-historical assumptions about Jesus as he actually was may really be existential-historical assertions about Jesus as he truly is, which is to say, as he is believed to be by those who bear witness to him, then it is always possible that just this is the case with anything that may be said or implied about Jesus' faith. But, then, the faith of Jesus is so far from being the condition of the christological assertion as to be conditioned by it, in the sense that what is said or implied about his faith is not by way of grounding this assertion but simply one of the ways of formulating it.

There seems no reason to doubt that material in the synoptic tradition that is usually classified as legendary is properly interpreted in exactly this way. Thus, whether one thinks of the temptation stories near the beginning of the gospels or of the scene in Gethsemane that they each recount toward the end (Matt. 4:1–11 par.; Mark 14:32–42), what is said or implied about Jesus' fidelity to his vocation or his submission to God's will is evidently by way of bearing witness to his decisive significance rather than adducing evidence sufficient to ground it. But so far as I can see, no good reason can be given why one should not suppose the same to be true of anything that may be said or implied anywhere in the New Testament about Jesus' godly fear and obedience (Heb. 5:7 ff.), his exemplary endurance of suffering (1 Pet. 2:21 ff.), or his sinlessness (Heb. 4:15, 7:26 ff.). On the contrary, the best of reasons have already been given in developing the preceding objection why one ought not to suppose anything else. Because the self-understanding of Jesus, like that of any other human being, could not have been experienced by those who came to believe in him and thus could not have even possibly been the ground of their christological formulations, such statements as they made or implied about his unique authenticity are themselves christological predications, not statements of their reasons for making such. No less than the accounts of his miraculous conception and birth or of his equally miraculous appearances after death, they are witness of faith and thus have a strictly existential-historical, not an empirical-historical, kind of meaning (Attridge; Nineham, 1977: 166–187).

But this is not the only objection to be made to the typical revisionary understanding of the conditions of christological predication once one orients oneself to the christologies of the New Testament. So far from providing support for such an understanding, these christologies in fact preclude it. This they do because, given their understanding of the christological assertion, Jesus' having perfectly actualized the possibility of authentic self-understanding is not even a necessary, much less the sufficient, condition of the truth of this assertion.

That this is so can be made clear by recalling what was said earlier about the predicates in terms of which the christologies of the New Testament are characteristically formulated. According to the analysis I offered of the christological question, the specific form of this question addressed by all of these christologies arises only at a certain level of theistic religious controversy. This is the level at which what is asked about is not only the identity of God, in the sense of the ultimate reality implicitly authorizing our authentic self-understanding, but also the identity of the decisive re-presentation of God, whereby the meaning of God for us is itself made fully explicit. Thus the honorific titles in terms of which the New Testament writers formulate the christological assertion, such as "Christ" or "Son of Man," "Lord" or "Son of God," are all ways of designating such a decisive re-presentation. And the same is true of the other main type of predicates characteristically found in the formulations of the New Testament—namely, the mythological qualifications of Jesus' origin and destiny and the legendary as well as mythological qualifications of the course of his life.

As far as the New Testament is concerned, then, whatever may be assumed about Jesus as he actually was, the one thing that must be asserted about him is who he truly is; and this means that, in some concepts and symbols or other, he must be asserted to be the decisive re-presentation of God, through whom God's own gift and demand become fully explicit, thereby authorizing our authentic understanding of ourselves.

We have already noted that the concepts and symbols in which this may be done cover a wide range of metaphysical differences, even in the case of the terms typically used in the christologies of the New Testament. Moreover, there can be little question that, when these christologies think and speak of Jesus as Son of God, they are so far from making the same metaphysical claim later made by the councils of Nicaea and Chalcedon that they may as well mean that Jesus is a human being whom God has appointed as that he is a divine being who has become man.

Yet we have also seen that even the most diverse concepts and symbols are functionally interchangeable insofar as they can all be used religiously to identify Jesus as the decisive re-presentation of God. Thus, whenever Jesus' appointment as Christ or Son of God is represented as taking place, whether at his resurrection, as in the sermons in Acts (2:32, 36, 5:31, 13:32 f.), or at his baptism, as in the Gospel of Mark (1:11), in either case he is asserted to be the one through whom God is decisively revealed. And the same is true of the "conception christology" that we find in the infancy narratives of Matthew's and Luke's gospels (Matt. 1–2; Luke 1–2), as well as of the "pre-existence christology" developed by Paul and John (Phil. 2:5 ff.; John 1:1–18). As contradictory as these latter types of christologies clearly are when considered metaphysically, both of one another and of the adoptionist christologies evident in Acts and Mark, they nevertheless serve to formulate one and the same christological assertion of Jesus' decisive significance for human existence (Brown, 1977: 29–32, 140–142).

Furthermore, because this is the assertion that all the New

Testament christologies intend to make, it clearly will not do to exaggerate their metaphysical differences from the christology of the later church councils. However "low" their formulations may seem to be when compared with the "high" christology of Nicaea and Chalcedon, it is quite misleading to suppose that the history of christology is anything like a development whereby one who begins by being thought and spoken about as man eventually comes to be represented as God. Although the earliest christology does indeed seem to have thought and spoken about Jesus in terms drawn from Jewish religious tradition, and hence as in every way human and in no way divine, the point of such thinking and speaking was nevertheless to place Jesus on the *divine* side of the relationship between God and human beings generally, not on the human side. As he whom God has made Messiah or Son of Man by raising him from the dead, Jesus is the one through whom God has spoken and acted in a final, decisive way, to judge and to save (K. Berger, 1970–71; 1973–74; Grillmeier: 9 ff.; Marshall: 128 f.). Thus, given the concepts and symbols in terms of which it is formulated, the claim made for Jesus even in this earliest Jewish-Christian christology was a maximal, not a minimal claim. It was not an exception to but rather an illustration of the truth that John Knox argues the whole history of christology will demonstrate—"that where a greater or a lesser name is proposed for Christ, it is always the greater that is adopted" (Knox, 1955: 80).

But if the claim made for Jesus by all the New Testament christologies is that he is the decisive re-presentation of God, in the sense of the one through whom the meaning of God for us is made fully explicit, his own self-understanding cannot be either a necessary or the sufficient condition of the truth of this claim. It cannot be a necessary condition any more than, in general, someone's belief in a claim can be a necessary condition of the claim's being true. To assert the truth of a claim is not to say or imply that someone believes it, but rather that it is worthy of being believed by everyone, whether anyone believes it or not (Ogden, 1977: 109–114). Likewise, to assert that Jesus is the decisive re-presentation of God is not to say or imply how Jesus *did* understand himself but rather how everyone *ought* to understand himself or herself, even if no one has ever done so or ever will do so. Therefore, however Jesus may have understood his existence, the assertion may still be true that he is the decisive re-presentation of God, because the self-understanding implicitly authorized by the ultimate reality called "God" is the very self-understanding explicitly authorized through Jesus.

But if Jesus' self-understanding cannot be a necessary condition of the characteristic claim of New Testament christologies, far less can it be the sufficient condition of making this claim. It lies in the nature of any self-understanding, even one that would be perfectly authentic, that it can be authorized as authentic only by a primal source beyond itself. In theistic religious terms, the name for this primal source is "God," understood as identifying ultimate reality in a certain way in its meaning for us, and thus as authorizing the authentic understanding of our existence. But we have also noted how in theistic religions the term "God" typically comes to be used more to *ask* the existential question than to *answer* it, insofar as the very thing that is taken to be questionable is the meaning of God for us. So it is that these religions also typically speak of some decisive re-presentation of God, whereby the meaning of God for us is made fully explicit. As such, however, this decisive re-presentation of God is different in principle from even a perfectly authentic self-understanding, being the primal source by which even it must be authorized—specifically, its *explicit* primal source, God being understood as the *implicit* primal source authorizing the same self-understanding.

But, as we have seen, the claim made for Jesus in some

terms or other by all the New Testament christologies is that he is just such a decisive re-presentation of the meaning of God for us (Grillmeier: 33). Consequently, so far from asserting merely that he perfectly actualized authentic self-understanding, they make the infinitely more exalted claim that he is the explicit primal source that alone can authorize any such self-understanding. To this extent, the fact that Jesus' understanding of himself was perfectly authentic, even if it could be established as a fact, would not be sufficient to support the claim that the writers of the New Testament characteristically make for him. The most it would allow one to say is that Jesus is the primary authority for all Christian faith and witness. But in their understanding, Jesus is not merely one authority among others, even the primary such authority; rather, he is the primal *source* of all authority made fully explicit, and hence not *an* authority at all in the same literal sense of the word (Ogden, 1976a; 1976b).

To be sure, revisionary christologies typically obscure this difference in principle between being even a primary religious authority and being the explicit primal source that authorizes it. This may be the easier for them to do because, in mythological or legendary representations, the explicit primal source of authority is commonly thought and spoken about as though it simply were an authority. Thus, in the Fourth Gospel, for example, Jesus as the decisive revealer is represented as having been sent by the Father and as speaking and acting solely with the Father's authorization. "For I have not spoken on my own authority; the Father who sent me has himself given me commandment what to say and what to speak. . . . What I say, therefore, I say as the Father has bidden me" (John 12:49 f.). The point of such representations, of course, is in no way to diminish Jesus' decisive significance, but rather to uphold it, as becomes clear when the Son who is represented as obediently doing the Father's will is also said to have the same power as the Father and to deserve the same honor (5:21–27). Even so, the very representation of Jesus as himself an authority authorized by God tends to obscure the analogical rather than literal sense in which this is certainly to be understood (Bultmann, 1965: 404). But for whatever reason, revisionary christologies that seek rather to reformulate incarnational doctrine than to replace it especially tend to argue that a human being whose self-understanding was perfectly authentic, and hence fully authorized by God, could hardly be merely human. Being perfectly open to God's gift and demand, he or she would be fully indwelt by God and so also perfectly divine (Rahner and Weger: 114 f.).

A definitive reply to this kind of argument, however, seems to me to have been given by John Hick in a criticism made some years ago of the christology of D. M. Baillie. Even today, Baillie's attempt to interpret the mystery of the incarnation as perfectly actualizing what he called "the paradox of grace" remains one of the most impressive examples of the type of revisionary christology I have been criticizing (D. M. Baillie: 117 f.). But as Hick effectively showed, one cannot suppose Baillie's attempt to succeed unless one allows incarnation to be defined simply as complete immanence or construes the "deity" claimed for Jesus by the ecumenical creeds as his merely "adjectival divinity." According to Hick, "when the Nicene symbol (followed by the Chalcedonian definition) speaks of Christ as ὁμοούσιος τῷ πατρί, it is obviously not meant that Jesus was divine in the same manner as other men, but in much fuller measure. For the point of insisting that the Son is ὁμοούσιος with the Father was that Jesus, and He alone, could win men's salvation. Faith in Jesus was faith not in a man but in God." Yet it is just this, Hick argued, that Baillie's christology ceases to assert when it claims that "the paradox of grace in perfect operation *is* incarnation." For "to think of the incarnation in such wise that any man who, divinely graced, lived a perfect human life, would thereby be

God incarnate, is to define incarnation in terms, not of deity, but of divinity adjectivally construed, and is to fail in the task of restating the faith of the creeds for the modern world" (Hick, 1958: 3, 10, 11).

Anyone still inclined to advance Baillie's kind of argument that one who is uniquely man of God simply *is* uniquely God in man may well ponder Hick's criticism (cf. Hick, 1966). But I take its essential point to allow of a less restrictive formulation than Hick gave it. While there does indeed seem to be a difference in principle between even perfectly actualizing authentic existence and being the incarnation of God asserted by Nicaea and Chalcedon, these are hardly the only terms in which what is really essential in this difference may be formulated. On the contrary, I have urged that even in the supposedly "low" christology of the earliest Jewish-Christian community, the claim made for Jesus was that he is the decisive re-presentation of God and as such belongs on the divine rather than on the human side of the relationship between God and human beings generally. But if I am right about this, the really essential difference, upheld in some terms or other by all New Testament christologies, is the difference between being merely one more authority, even the primary such authority, and being the explicit primal source from which all authority derives. Because even a perfectly authentic human existence need be no more than one authority among others, on the same level as ourselves, even if first and foremost among us, Jesus' having actualized such an existence cannot possibly be the sufficient condition of the truth of these christologies. For the essential claim made by each of them, whatever the concepts and symbols in which it was formulated, is that Jesus is rather the primal source of all authority, on the same level as God, even if also distinct from God as this very source now become fully explicit.

So much, then, for the objections that can be made to the third point in the revisionary consensus. If they are anything like as serious as I take them to be, then at this point also the typical revisionary christology is so problematic as to be untenable. But if we cannot give this answer to our question about the conditions of christological predication, how we are to answer it should have already become apparent from the preceding discussion.

I have argued that, because the question christology answers is an existential-historical question, the assertion that constitutes christology explicitly as such must be an existential-historical assertion. Specifically, it is an assertion of the meaning of Jesus for us, or, to be more precise, of the decisive significance of Jesus for human existence. Thus any appropriate christological predication is by way of asserting, in some conceptuality and symbolism or other, that Jesus is the decisive re-presentation of God, in the sense of the one through whom the meaning of God for us, and hence the meaning of ultimate reality for us, becomes fully explicit. But if this is the constant function of even the most variable christological predicates, it is not difficult to specify the conditions that must be satisfied if any of them is to be truthfully asserted. The only necessary and, therefore, the sufficient condition of any such assertion is that the meaning of ultimate reality for us that is always already presented implicitly in our very existence be just that meaning of God for us that is re-presented explicitly through Jesus.

This means, on the one hand, that Jesus is truthfully said to be Christ, or any of the other things he is appropriately said or implied to be, if, but only if, the ultimate reality that implicitly authorizes the authentic understanding of our existence is the one who is explicitly revealed through Jesus to be God. This, we may say, is the *metaphysical* aspect of the condition that has to be satisfied if the christological assertion is to be true in any of its formulations. In this aspect, the condition can be known to be satisfied only by way of properly metaphysical inquiry into the structure of ultimate reality in itself. For, as we have seen, it is only insofar as ultimate reality in itself has one structure instead of another that it can have the meaning for us it is re-presented as having through Jesus, who explicitly reveals it to be God.

But the same condition also has another aspect that, following our earlier discussion, we may distinguish as *moral.* Thus, on the other hand, Jesus is truthfully said to be what any christological formulation appropriately asserts or implies him to be if, but only if, the understanding of our existence that is implicitly authorized by what is ultimately real is the self-understanding that is explicitly authorized through Jesus as faith in God. In this aspect, the condition of the christological assertion can also be known to be satisfied through properly moral inquiry into how one is to act in relation to one's fellow beings. For, as we have also seen, it is only insofar as acting in one way instead of another is how one ought to act in relation to one's fellows that ultimate reality can have the meaning for us it is re-presented as having through Jesus, who explicitly authorizes faith in God as our authentic self-understanding.

Thus to argue, however, is clearly to affirm that the condition of asserting a christological predicate has a historical as well as an existential and therefore moral and metaphysical aspect. Consequently, it is in no way to imply that the truth of the christological assertion could already be deduced simply from premises that are properly moral and metaphysical. I do indeed believe that there is and must be such a thing as an "a priori" or "transcendental" christology, insofar as the existential question of the ultimate meaning of human existence implies the notion of a decisive answer to this question, and any properly moral or metaphysical inquiry, if sufficiently pursued, more or less clearly forms the corresponding concept. Moreover, I understand it to belong to the very essence of the Christian witness to attest that the fundamental option for salvation that is decisively re-presented solely through Jesus is also implicitly presented to every human being as soon and as long as he or she exists humanly at all (Ogden, 1975a; 1979b). But if this means that I too affirm in my own way what Karl Rahner calls a "seeking christology" and the possibility of an "anonymous Christianity," I in no way deny the difference between a christology that seeks and one that has found or between a Christianity that remains nameless and one that is properly so-called (Rahner and Thüsing: 20–24, 59–69; Rahner, 1976: 206–211). Quite the contrary, I insist, as I have already insisted in an earlier chapter, that even the christological question, not to mention the assertion that answers it, logically could not be simply existential. Because it could not even arise except on the basis of particular experience of Jesus, it is and must be historical as well as existential, and the truth of the christological assertion that answers it could only be an a posteriori, not an a priori, kind of truth. Accordingly, the condition of making this assertion truthfully also has a historical aspect, in which it can be known to be satisfied only by properly historical, which is to say, empirical-historical, inquiry.

But as important as it is to insist on this, it is just as important to be clear that the empirical-historical inquiry that is required to justify the credibility of christological formulations is exactly the same as that which is required to justify their appropriateness. In the one respect, just as in the other, what is necessary is not a quest of the historical Jesus, but rather a quest of the earliest Christian witness. To assert any christological predicate of Jesus naturally requires that the condition of truthfully asserting it of any subject must be satisfied by the particular subject Jesus. But the conclusion reached in the preceding chapter was that the Jesus who is the real subject of the christological assertion is the Jesus attested by the earliest Christian witness. This means that the condition of truthfully making this assertion in any of its formulations lies not in the being of Jesus in himself that we still have to infer from this witness, but rather in the meaning of Jesus for us that this witness itself already normatively represents. Consequently, it is by way of empirical-historical inquiry into what is meant by Jesus in this normative witness that the condition of asserting any christological predicate truthfully can be known to be satisfied, insofar as this can be historically known at all.

5. The Quest for Freedom and the Witness of the Apostles

At the outset of our inquiry I distinguished two main tasks with which we would be concerned during the course of it. In the first place, there is the more constructive task of *making* the point of christology in the way in which a christology of reflection, as distinct from the christology of witness on which it reflects, is supposed to do. In the second place, there is the more critical task of *talking about* the point of christology, which for us today is doubly imperative, given the difficulties now apparent not only in traditional christology but in most revisionary christology as well.

Up to this point we have been engaged by and large with the second and more critical of these two tasks. By considering in some detail each of the three points in what I have called "the contemporary revisionary consensus," we have carried out something like a Heideggerian "dismantling" *(Destruktion)* of the usual revisionary christology (Heidegger: 19–27). That is to say, we have tried to return from the whole long tradition of christological reflection, of which contemporary christologies are typically the revision, to the original experience underlying the constitutive christological assertion. In this way we have tried to recover the point of this assertion, so as to give an adequate account of its meaning and truth. Thus we have asked about the *question* to which it is the answer, the *subject* about whom it is the assertion, and the conditions that must be satisfied in order for any *predicate* appropriately used in formulating it to be truthfully asserted. If one result of this effort has been to demonstrate that the typical revisionary christology is more of a problem than a solution, its other result, insofar as it has been successful, has been to establish the possibility of a revisionary alternative that is not similarly problematic.

Specifically, we have established, first of all, that the question christology answers can be understood not simply as a question about Jesus, but also and at the same time as a question about the meaning of ultimate reality for human existence. As such, it is an existential-historical question that asks not about the being of Jesus in himself, but about the meaning of Jesus for us, given our more fundamental question about the meaning of ultimate reality for us, and hence about the authentic understanding of our existence. Reasoning, then, that the assertion that answers this question can only be an existential-historical assertion, we have further established that the subject of this assertion can be understood not as the so-called historical Jesus, or, in my term, the empirical-historical Jesus, but rather as the existential-historical Jesus. This means that the Jesus who is said to be Christ is not someone whom we first come to know only more or less probably by way of inference from the earliest Christian witness, but rather the one whom we already know most certainly precisely through this earliest witness as its primal authorizing source. Finally, we have established that the conditions of asserting a christological predicate in no way require that Jesus must have perfectly actualized the possibility of authentic self-understanding. On the contrary, because the function of any christological predicate is to assert somehow that Jesus is the decisive re-presentation of the meaning of God for us, and hence of the meaning of ultimate reality for us, the only condition of truthfully asserting it is satisfied if the God whose gift and demand are made fully explicit through Jesus is indeed what is ultimately real and if the possibility of faith in this God that Jesus explicitly authorizes is indeed our authentic possibility as human beings.

But as important as it certainly is to have shown that one can talk about the point of christology without becoming involved in the problems typical of revisionary christologies, there remains the first and more constructive task of actually making the point of christology at once appropriately and credibly in our situation today. Of course, to talk about the point of christology as we have been doing is already in a way to make it, just as, conversely, to make the point of christology in the reflective way in which we must now try to make it is impossible without talking about it. Even so, the more constructive christological task that we have set for ourselves requires that we now go beyond all that we have so far succeeded in establishing. There are two main reasons for this, both of which have to do with the situation in which we today must develop a constructive christology of reflection.

I stated in the introductory chapter that such a christology can be adequate only insofar as, in our present situation, it is credible as well as appropriate, in that it answers for the truth as well as the meaning of the christology of witness. Presupposed by this statement is my view that a christology of reflection, involving as it does the same human understanding involved in any other kind of critical reflection, is exactly like everything else human in being thoroughly conditioned both socially and culturally. On this view christological reflection always and of necessity takes place in some particular historical situation, in terms of its agenda of problems and of its resources for clarifying and solving them. Consequently, while the demand remains constant that any adequate christological claim must be supported by reasons sufficient to establish both its appropriateness and its credibility, exactly what this demand requires is also always variable in that it is a function of different historical situations. In this sense the two criteria of christological reflection are in an important respect situation-dependent as well as situation-invariant; and because this is so, reasons that would be sufficient to establish either the appropriateness or the credibility of a christological claim in one situation may very well not be sufficient to do so in another.

Unless I am mistaken, our situation today strikingly illustrates this general rule about the situation-dependence of the criteria of christological reflection. Because of changes in the situation in which we must now ask about the meaning and the truth of the christology of witness, the adequacy of our answers to these questions must be judged by criteria whose specific requirements are correspondingly changed. Even though now as before christological claims must indeed be both appropriate and credible, just what it means for them to be either is in part new and different because the same is true of the situation in which we must now try to formulate them.

Consider, first of all, the changes in our situation that have made for partly new and different requirements with respect to the *credibility* of christological claims. It is generally recognized that the whole history of modern theology in the West has been decisively determined by the modern quest for freedom and the secular culture that is at once the outcome and the instrument of this quest. Crucial for such secular culture has been the rise of modern science and the closely related development of a science-based technology. Thanks to the first, our outlook as Western men and women has become increasingly dominated by the new scientific picture of the world, even as we owe to the second a new resolve to make use of our growing scientific knowledge and technical skill to emancipate ourselves and our fellows by transforming the natural and social conditions of our lives. Moreover, of a piece with both of these changes has been a growing historical consciousness, in the sense of an explicit awareness that human beings create themselves and one another by creating their own social and cultural orders and that to be fully and truly human is to be an active subject of such collective self-creation and not merely its passive object. The upshot of all these changes has been to pose the question of the credibility of the Christian witness in the sharpest possible way. One effect of historical consciousness is to deprive all appeals to mere authority of any save a strictly provisional validity. At the same time, a scientific world-picture directly questions the prescientific claims expressed or implied by all traditional witness and theology, even as an emancipatory resolve to transform the conditions of human existence expressly challenges the social and cultural orders for which such witness and theology have only too often functioned to provide the ultimate sanction.

Of course, it is no news that the modern quest for freedom and secular culture have posed a complex challenge to traditional Christianity. The warfare of science with theology is a familiar story to all of us, and no one knowledgeable of either the bourgeois revolutions of the eighteenth century or the proletarian revolutions of the twentieth needs to be informed of the extent to which their self-understandings have been explicitly atheistic and anti-Christian. Furthermore, we all recognize that Christian theologians have long since attempted to come to terms with this challenge, the history of revisionary theology in its succeeding phases—liberal, neo-orthodox, and postliberal—being above all the history of this attempt. And yet as true as this all is, there still seems reason to claim that the dominant expressions of this revisionary theology in Europe and North America have typically responded to one aspect of this challenge rather more successfully than they have to another. In fact, notwithstanding the theologies of the "social gospel," whose significance I should not wish to underestimate, the most influential expressions of revisionary theology all along have commonly been preoccupied more with theoretical questions of belief and truth than with practical issues of action and justice.

That this is so is not the least of the insights that we owe to the theologies of liberation that have recently begun to make an impact on our Western theological discussion. I myself have been particularly struck by the comparison Gustavo Gutiérrez draws on this very point. He argues that, whereas much contemporary theology seeks to respond to the challenge of the *"non-believer"* who questions our *"religious world"* as Christians, in a continent like Latin America the primary challenge is put to us rather by the *"non-person"* who, being excluded from active participation in the existing social and cultural order, questions us about our *"economic, social, political and cultural world"* (Gutiérrez: 37). I find this comparison extremely revealing, not only as to my own preoccupations as a theologian, but also as to those of European and North American theologians generally. Certainly for those of us who do our theology primarily in the academic context, the challenge to which we have been most concerned to respond is the more theoretical challenge posed by the typical modern nonbeliever, whom we are likely to know only too well among our colleagues in the other schools and departments of the universities and colleges in which we do our work. To be sure, the tradition of social Christianity has continued to be an influence even on academic theology in North America, and already during the 1960s Roman Catholic as well as Protestant theologians in Europe were contributing to the emergence of a new "political theology" (Baum; Bennett; Metz; Peukert [ed.]). But until very recently at any rate, most Western theologians appear to have been concerned primarily with the theoretical challenge to the truth of traditional religious belief that has arisen from the conflicting truth claims of modern secular culture and its secularistic self-interpretations (Rahner [ed.]: 123–143, 170 f.).

Gutiérrez and other liberation theologians can help us to

understand that the challenge of the nonbeliever can no longer be the only challenge to which a revisionary christology must seek to respond. There is also the challenge of the nonperson—of the one who finds the traditional christology of witness incredible, not because it is implicated in a religious world that for a small minority of men and women has now become untrue, but because it is implicated in an economic, social, political, and cultural world that for a vast majority of men and women continues to be unjust.

The difficulty with all analyses of our theological situation in terms of the problems created for the Christian witness by modern secularity is that they tend to overlook that the overwhelming majority of human beings, in our own more fully developed society as well as in other rather less developed ones, have benefitted only marginally from the vaunted progress of the modern West. So far from overcoming the classism of premodern societies, the rapid social changes involved in the development of modern technical civilization have merely transformed static inequalities into dynamic ones. Nor is this the only respect in which most men and women continue to be more the victims of historical process than its agents. If classism continues to divide human beings into oppressors and oppressed, the same is true of racism and sexism, nationalism and, if one may say so, culturalism as well. But what makes all this theologically problematic is the way in which the Christian witness of faith continues to be implicated in these fundamental divisions within the human community. Positively or negatively, it continues to provide an ultimate sanction for the injustices and oppressions of the existing social and cultural order. Thus, for anyone who in one or more respects is excluded from this order and who to this extent is a nonperson, there is indeed a problem with the credibility of the Christian witness. Only this problem is by no means merely theoretical but is eminently and urgently practical.

In my judgment, we now have every reason to recognize that the quest for freedom on which humanity today is embarked has this urgently practical as well as a more strictly theoretical aspect. It is not only a quest for truth in the sense of freedom from ignorance and error, it is also a quest for justice in the sense of freedom from want and oppression. But this means that if a christology of reflection is to be truly credible to persons engaged in this quest, it cannot rely solely on methods devised to vindicate the theoretical credibility of the christology of witness. Rather, it must devise new methods specifically designed to show that this witness remains practically credible as well even in face of a distinctively contemporary quest for justice.

What I mean by this can perhaps best be indicated for our present purposes by briefly developing a parallel that I have found increasingly illumining as I have thought about this problem of theological method. I contended in the introductory chapter that one of the aims of any revisionary christology must be so to formulate the point of the christology of witness as to demythologize it consistently and without remainder. By this I mean essentially what Rudolf Bultmann meant in proposing the theological method of radical demythologizing. This implies that I should also urge the adoption of something very like Bultmann's method of existentialist interpretation. For while one may indeed think of demythologizing and existentialist interpretation for certain purposes as two distinct methods, one is well advised to keep in mind that, in Bultmann's understanding, the word "demythologizing" is but a way of designating negatively one and the same hermeneutical procedure that the phrase "existentialist interpretation" serves to designate positively. But if this procedure is essential to vindicating the theoretical credibility of the christology of witness in our situation today, I should maintain that a closely parallel procedure is now required to vindicate its practical credibility. Specifically, an adequate christology of reflection now requires that one also follow a procedure whose negative and positive aspects can be designated respectively as "deideologizing" and "political interpretation."

By "deideologizing" I mean the method of so interpreting the meaning of the christology of witness as to disengage it from the economic, social, political, and cultural world whose injustices it is used, negatively if not positively, to sanction. This presupposes, naturally, a definite meaning for the word "ideology." In this meaning, the word designates a more or less comprehensive understanding of human existence, of how to exist and act as a human being, that functions to justify the interests of a particular group or individual by representing these interests as the demands of disinterested justice. Thus, by its very nature the actual effect of an ideology, if not its real intention, is to rationalize particular interests, even though it represents such interests in terms of universal justice. But this would seem to mean, then, that, insofar as the interests an ideology functions to justify are not, in fact, just, it itself provides the criterion for critically interpreting them by its own representation of them as just demands.

Readers who remember Bultmann's argument for demythologizing will have no difficulty recognizing the analogy I am suggesting between this understanding of ideology and Bultmann's understanding of myth. Even as, in his account, the real intention of myth to express the truth of human existence in relation to ultimate reality provides the criterion for demythologizing it, in the sense of eliminating its claims insofar as they are not empirically true, so, in the present account, the real representation by ideology of the demands of justice in human relations provides the criterion for deideologizing it, in the sense of eliminating its demands insofar as they are not universally just. Nor is this the full extent of the analogy that I am suggesting. For if Bultmann could further support the method of demythologizing by arguing that the New Testament writings themselves do not make use of myth primarily in order to advance empirical claims, but rather to set forth the understanding of human existence implied by the Christian witness, it seems to me one can give an analogous reason for employing the method of deideologizing. It is arguable at any rate that the primary use of ideology in the New Testament is not to justify the interests of some human beings against the just interests of others, but rather to give concrete content to Christian moral responsibility by making clear that it has to do precisely with establishing justice in human relations (Furnish, 1979; Ogden, 1981).

So far as the other method of "political interpretation" is concerned, suffice it to say that it consists in explicating the implications of the Christian witness for the specifically political aspect of moral responsibility. The key word here, obviously, is "politics," and in understanding its meaning I follow the lead of Reinhold Niebuhr, according to whom "the very essence of politics is the achievement of justice through equilibria of power." If this means, as Niebuhr explains, that "the central problem of politics is the problem of justice," it also implies that "politics always aims at some kind of a harmony or balance of interest" and that "politics is always a contest of power" (Davis and Good [eds.]: 143, 174, 193, 206). Assuming some such understanding of politics as Niebuhr thus sets forth, one may say that the specifically political aspect of moral responsibility involves the use of power to establish justice not only in the state and government but also throughout the whole social and cultural order—namely, by either maintaining or transforming all of the basic structures of this order so that each person is equally free with every other to be the active subject of his or her own self-creation, instead of being merely the passive object of the self-creations of others. Accordingly, a political interpretation of the christology of witness, which would be the positive meaning of deideologizing it, would make clear that the moral implications of this witness essentially include just such a specifically political responsibility for the basic structures of society and culture.

There will be occasion in the concluding chapter to argue further for the appropriateness of this kind of political interpretation by showing why it becomes a demand of the Christian witness itself, given a contemporary understanding of the scope of human power and responsibility. Meanwhile, I am concerned to insist on the necessity of such a theological method, along with the closely related method of deideologizing, if the christology of witness is to be credibly interpreted and formulated in the present situation. Whatever may have been the case in earlier situations to justify ignoring this necessity—and one suspects that even then it was more readily explained by the class bias of theologians than justified by their proper task—there is no excuse for us today to ignore that the criterion of credibility that any adequate christology of reflection must be concerned to satisfy has a practical as well as a theoretical aspect. Because the freedom for which responsible men and women are now searching involves the demand for justice as well as the demand for truth, we cannot hope to make the Christian witness fully credible to them unless we seek to meet the first of these demands as earnestly as we seek to meet the second. This is why, to the revisionary aim of consistently demythologizing the christology of witness, we must now add, as a further revisionary aim, consistently deideologizing it.

But if the specific requirements of credibility are to this extent new and different in the present situation, they are not the only such requirements of which this must be said. A christology of reflection must be appropriate as well as credible, and with respect to the other criterion of *appropriateness* as well ours is in part a changed situation that demands a corresponding change in its specific requirements. Of course, in this respect also it is important not to exaggerate the extent of the change. If the specific requirements of credibility have always been more or less controversial in theology—and historical study abundantly confirms that they have—the same is true of the specific requirements of appropriateness. Consequently, aside from the fact that the demand for appropriateness as such is as unchanged now as it has ever been, there likewise is nothing new or different about the fact that there is by no means any consensus about just what this demand requires. And yet if the fact of controversy about its requirements is hardly new, the precise nature of the controversy has recently become in certain respects significantly different. This can be made clear by considering the basic question raised by the demand for appropriateness and the different main types of answers that are most commonly given to this question.

The basic question that the demand for appropriateness raises is, of course, What is the standard or norm by which the appropriateness of witness and theology is to be measured? Traditionally, Protestant theology has answered this question by pointing to "scripture alone" as the primary standard or norm of such appropriateness. To be sure, this so-called scriptural principle has been variously understood throughout Protestant history even by the types of Protestantism in which, unlike liberal Protestantism, it has typically been upheld—from the classical Protestantism of the Reformers through Protestant orthodoxy on down to the neo-orthodoxy of our own century. But even if the exact meaning of *sola scriptura* has been controversial among Protestants, it has nevertheless served to define one main type of answer to the basic question as over against a second main type of answer traditionally given by Roman Catholic theology in the principle "scripture and tradition." Here too different types of Roman Catholicism have understood this principle in different ways—from the Council of Trent through the First Vatican Council to the Second. But, again, there is an essential unity in these several ways insofar as they all insist that the primary standard or norm of the appropriateness of Christian witness and theology is not only the canon of scripture but also the tradition of the church, which is to say, finally, its *magisterium,* or teaching office, whereby even scripture itself receives its only authoritative interpretation.

Finally, there is a third main type of answer to the basic question that was first worked out by liberal Protestantism. As I already indicated, liberal Protestants typically abandoned *sola scriptura,* replacing it with the principle that the real standard or norm of appropriateness is Jesus himself— the so-called historical Jesus, who for this reason is the object of a critical, analytical quest behind the tradition of the church, including the tradition canonized in the New Testament. In this case also there were alternative ways within liberal Protestantism of understanding this principle, some of which were at least verbally close enough to the other types of Protestantism to be difficult to classify. Moreover, something very like the same type of answer also came to be given by certain Roman Catholic theologians belonging to the general trend within Catholic theology usually identified as Modernism. But however nuanced or widespread, the answer to the basic question of the appropriateness of Christian witness and theology motivating the original quest of the historical Jesus was a third type of answer, clearly different from the other two. The purpose of this original quest, whatever the purposes of those who have continued to appeal to the historical Jesus, was not to support the authority of either scripture or tradition but rather to replace it (Ogden, 1976b).

These, then, are the three main types of answer that are usually given to the question of the standard or norm of appropriateness. If even they make clear why there certainly is no consensus in answering this question, they still do not exhaust the answers that can be given to it, nor do they include the answer that, in my opinion, has the greatest claim on our acceptance today. As a matter of fact, the very development that makes it possible as well as necessary to give a quite different answer to the question renders all three of these usual ways of answering it doubtfully tenable in the present situation.

I refer to the ongoing development of historical-critical study of scripture, especially of the New Testament. As a result of such study, it is now generally recognized by exegetes and historians of early Christian literature that every writing in the New Testament canon depends upon sources, oral if not also written, expressing a witness to Jesus earlier than its own. Thus, in the case of the synoptic gospels, for instance, first source-critical analysis and then form and redaction criticism have made possible the reconstruction of a complex history of tradition lying behind the composition of our canonical gospels. This history of the synoptic tradition is now so widely acknowledged, indeed, that even the Pontifical Biblical Commission of the Roman Catholic Church, in an instruction on the historical truth of the gospels in 1964, has allowed that "to judge properly concerning the reliability of what is transmitted in the Gospels, the interpreter should pay diligent attention to the three stages of tradition by which the doctrine and the life of Jesus have come down to us"—the three stages referred to being, in the words of the instruction, "the ministry of Jesus," "the preaching of the apostles," and "the writing by the evangelists" (Brown, 1975: 112 f.). So also, then, with the other New Testament writings, all of which have likewise been disclosed by source-critical, form-critical, or tradition-critical analysis to be in their respectively different ways interpretations and formulations of yet earlier Christian traditions, either oral or written or both.

The effect of this disclosure with respect to the whole question of the norm of appropriateness is twofold. In the first

place, it completely undercuts just that clear distinction between scripture and tradition on which both the traditional
Protestant and the traditional Roman Catholic answers to the
question in their different ways depend. From the Catholic
standpoint, the objection to the Protestant answer has always
been that it is arbitrary, given that the New Testament canon
is, after all, a creation of the early church, and thus itself a
product of tradition. Hence to acknowledge the authority of
scripture as thus canonized is *eo ipso* to acknowledge the
authority of tradition; and to then want to restrict such authority solely to the church that created the canon has all the
marks of arbitrariness if not outright inconsistency. The traditional Protestant reply to this objection has been to deny
that the early church created the canon in the sense the
objection presupposes. While the early church did indeed
formally acknowledge and declare that the writings of the
New Testament are the sole primary authority in the church,
it did not itself thereby constitute the canon. Rather, it sub-
mitted its own judgments concerning the writings to be included in the canon to independent criteria—in the final
analysis, "the criterion of apostolicity" (Pelikan: 114; Knox,
1952: 66 f.). It declared that only those writings could be
reckoned as having primary authority which expressed the
original and originating witness of the apostles. Yet as we
have seen, the whole effect of recent study of the New Testament is to disclose that none of the writings included within
it is an apostolic writing in this strict sense of the word. On
the contrary, if they are now judged by this same criterion,
the New Testament writings themselves are one and all precisely tradition, in that they are each a later interpretation
and formulation in a changed historical situation of some
earlier stage or stages of Christian witness.

But if the first effect of historical study is thus to break
down the distinction between scripture and tradition, which
the traditional Protestant and the traditional Catholic an-

swers both presuppose, it also has the effect of rendering the third main type of answer considerably more questionable than it was once thought to be. The very methods of analysis —source-critical, form-critical, tradition-critical—that have disclosed the gospels themselves to be really tradition, have also confirmed that even the earliest stratum of witness now accessible to us by critical analysis of the gospels is itself witness to Jesus, as distinct from Jesus' own words and deeds. Thus, if the Pontifical Biblical Commission still refers to the first stage in the synoptic tradition as "the ministry of Jesus," thereby begging the question, a critic like Bultmann knows to speak of it more cautiously simply as "old tradition" (Bultmann, 1965: 2). To be sure, we have already noted in an earlier chapter that this is in the first instance a literary conclusion about the traditions redacted in the gospels, not a historical judgment about what can or cannot be known by making use of these traditions as sources. It means simply that even our earliest possible sources about Jesus are all secondary and that even these earliest sources all have the character of engaged witnesses of faith rather than disinterested historical reports (Nineham, 1977: 89 ff.). But even if this still allows for the possibility of using these sources for an empirical-historical inquiry concerning what Jesus himself actually said and did, there can be little question that it renders all such inquiry peculiarly problematic. In the nature of the case, one can avoid begging the question in reaching conclusions about Jesus only by acknowledging that the only evidence one ever has for any such conclusion is what is said or implied about Jesus in the earliest stratum of Christian witness that we are now in a position to reconstruct. This inevitably raises the question whether the historical Jesus, as distinct from the Jesus attested by this earliest Christian witness, can still be plausibly regarded as the norm for judging the appropriateness of all Christian witness and theology.

Of course, it will also be clear from preceding chapters that this is not the only serious question that can be asked about this third typical understanding of the norm of appropriateness. There is also the question—to my mind, far more serious—whether the very attempt to understand Jesus himself as this norm does not implicitly deny the characteristic claim that the Christian witness makes about him by its christological assertion. Even the primary norm of appropriateness can be no more than one authority among others, as distinct from the primal source of authority by which even the primary norm alone is authorized. But what does it mean to assert that Jesus is the Christ, or any of the other things that Christians have historically asserted him to be, if not precisely that Jesus is just such a primal authorizing source, and hence infinitely more than any authority derived from this source, even the primary such authority? I submit that the deeper difficulty with the typically liberal theological answer to the question of the norm of appropriateness is that it assigns to Jesus himself, contrary to the clear intention of the apostolic witness, the role that rightly belongs rather to the apostles.

If this is so, however, the way to respond to the challenge posed by the ongoing development of historical-critical study of the New Testament is not by abandoning the early church's criterion of apostolicity. Quite the contrary, if Jesus is rightly asserted by the Christian witness to be infinitely more than any norm, because he is the primal source of all norms made fully explicit, then the early church was exactly right in taking apostolicity to be the criterion of canonicity. It lies in the very logic of the concept of "authority" that the primal *source* of authority, whether implicit or explicit, cannot itself be *an* authority, at least in the same literal sense of the word. On the other hand, and by the same logic, there belongs to the original authority authorized by its primal source, and so in this case to the witness of the apostles as explicitly authorized by Jesus, the unique role of also being the originating authority and therefore the sole primary norm or canon. This is so because it is solely through this original and originating authority that the primal source authorizing it is explicitly available precisely as such.

In other words, the two concepts of "primary authority" and "primal authorizing source" are correlative concepts in that each may and must be defined in relation to the other. This puts in somewhat different terms the same point that John Knox characteristically expresses in speaking of "the Church and the reality of Christ": "One way of describing the Church is to say that it is the community which remembers Jesus; but one can equally truly define Jesus (in the only really significant meaning of that name for the Christian) as the one who is remembered. It is only as he is remembered that he has meaning for either Christian theology or Christian devotion. . . . the human existence of Jesus, insofar as it has continuing being and importance, is a memory of the Church" (Knox, 1962: 49; 1957–58: 57). Similarly, I am saying, if the primary authority of the apostles may and must be described as deriving entirely from Jesus as its primal authorizing source, Jesus himself may and must be defined (in the only really significant meaning of "Jesus" for Christian faith and witness) as the explicit primal source whence the original and originating witness of the apostles derives its primary authority.

But this is to say that what we today have reason to regard as mistaken in the early church's creation of the New Testament canon is not its criterion of canonicity, which was exactly right, but only the historical judgments it made in its own efforts to apply this criterion. Given the historical methods and results now available to us, the original and originating witness of the apostles, and hence the canon or norm of appropriateness, can and must be relocated—namely, from the writings of the New Testament as such, which are precisely not apostolic in the relevant sense, to the earliest stratum of Christian witness that we today can reconstruct, using the New Testament writings as our primary historical sources (Ogden, 1976a; 1976b).

We shall see in the next chapter that this alternative answer to the question of the norm of appropriateness is by no means unrelated to the typical answer of liberal theology and to the quest of the historical Jesus that this answer originally motivated. In fact, we shall discover that it is precisely the methods and results to which the continuing pursuit of this quest has now led, in the form of the so-called new quest of the historical Jesus, that make it possible for us today to relocate the canon in accordance with the early church's own criterion of apostolicity. For our purposes here, however, the important point is simply that the alternative answer for which I have argued is necessary in our theological situation today—that with respect to the second criterion of appropriateness also the specific requirements we must satisfy if our constructive christology of reflection is to be adequate are in part new and different. As sufficient as it may have been in earlier situations to appeal simply to the New Testament to establish the appropriateness of christological claims, we now have to face up to the insufficiency of any such procedure. This is so, at any rate, if we still wish to maintain that apostolicity is the only proper criterion of canonicity, and hence of the appropriateness of all Christian witness and theology. Provided we are unwilling to surrender at least this much of the traditional Protestant scriptural principle, there is simply nothing else for us to do. Assuming the best historical methods and knowledge available in our situation, we clearly have to decide either for a traditional New Testament canon that we can no longer justify by the early church's own criterion of apostolicity or else for this same criterion of apostolicity, which now allows us to justify only a nontraditional canon.

My contention is that the second of these two options is by far the better, and I have tried to indicate the reasons for this by arguing that the early church's criterion of apostolicity is exactly right. In any event, it is this option with respect to theological method or procedure that also helps to determine the shape of the constructive christology of reflection toward which these chapters are directed. Even as we can now vindicate the claim of the christology of witness to be credible only by taking full account of the quest for freedom in its practical as well as its theoretical aspect, so we can now establish the christology of witness as appropriate only by appealing to the witness of the apostles as something distinct from the canon of the New Testament.

Such, as I see them, are the demands of our situation. Whether one can fully meet them and thus achieve an adequate christology of reflection is the question we shall try to answer in succeeding chapters.

6. Jesus Who Is Said to Be Christ

The task before us in this second part of the book is to contribute toward a constructive christology of reflection that will be credible as well as appropriate, given the demands of our present situation. More specifically, my argument is directed toward developing what I shall speak of henceforth as a christology of liberation. Part of what I have in mind in speaking in these terms was a major theme of the last chapter, in which we sought to take account of the modern quest for freedom and the difference it makes with respect to the specific requirements of credibility that our reflection will have to satisfy. We learned that responsible men and women today are typically concerned not only with theoretical questions of belief and truth, but also with practical issues of action and justice, with the result that what they are prepared to regard as credible tends to have an urgently practical as well as a merely theoretical aspect. Because the freedom they seek for themselves and their fellow human beings is a freedom from want and oppression as well as from ignorance and error, they are not likely to find any claim really credible that functions positively or negatively to maintain existing orders of injustice.

Yet as important as these considerations certainly are in understanding the specific requirements of credibility that christology today has to meet, they hardly seem to explain why it has to be a christology of liberation. To understand this, we have to take account of the further fact that it is precisely the concern for freedom that is above all *the* contemporary human concern—or, to put the same point more exactly, it is precisely the concept or symbol of "freedom" in terms of which men and women today above all articulate their deepest concern as human beings. Of course, what they more immediately have in mind in speaking of freedom is typically just such secular freedoms from want and oppression as well as from ignorance and falsehood as set the limits of what they regard as credible. But even if the freedom they ultimately seek is conceived to be nothing more than such worldly well-being, the significant point, so far as christology is concerned, is that it is precisely in terms of freedom that they typically conceive what is of ultimate concern to them. This means that it is in the very same terms of freedom that christology also must think and speak if it is to address the existential question implied by their concern. Even if the answer christology has to give to this question is, in critical respects, radically different from any merely secular freedom, unless it is formulated in terms in which men and women are now asking this question, it is not likely even to be understood, much less accepted as worth believing (Ogden, 1979a).

If this explains why a christology of liberation is necessary today, there may well appear to be reasons why such a christology is also possible. As distinctive as the contemporary quest for freedom doubtless is, there is hardly anything new either about men and women seeking liberation from various forms of bondage or about their making use of the concept or symbol of "freedom" to give expression to their deepest concern as human beings. On the contrary, the quest for liberation in one form or another seems to be universally human, and in any number of religious and cultural traditions the goal of ultimate transformation has been thought and spoken of precisely in terms of freedom. This was true, indeed, in the very milieu of Hellenistic syncretism in which the church that produced the writings of the New Testament to a large extent elaborated its own christological reflections. Mainly for this reason no doubt, but also presumably because they were convinced that the traditional christology of witness could be appropriately formulated in such terms, both Paul and John already confirmed the possibility of a christology of liberation by using the Stoic concept of "freedom" (ἐλευθερία) in some of their own christological formulations (Schlier: 492–500).

To be sure, we ought not to exaggerate the importance of such a christology even for these two New Testament theologians. As far as John is concerned, there is only one brief passage in which he expressly speaks of Jesus in terms of freedom—namely, the verses in the eighth chapter where he has Jesus tell those who have believed in him, "If you continue in my word, you are truly my disciples, and you will know the truth, and the truth will make you free," and "if the Son makes you free, you will be free indeed" (vv. 31 f., 36). Even if what is here said or implied about Jesus is entirely in keeping with John's other, more fully elaborated formulations, it is hardly justification for interpreting his christology as a whole as a christology of liberation. The case of Paul is rather different, because the concept of "freedom" and its various cognates play a much more prominent role in his whole understanding of Christian existence. And yet even in Paul's case, one must keep in mind that it is really only in the Letter to the Galatians that he expressly speaks of Jesus as liberator and that even there his other most explicit christological formulations (1:4, 2:20, 3:13, 4:4 f.) do not make any use of the concept of freedom (Betz: 255).

Still, even if we fully recognize this, there can be no question that Paul does expressly speak of the work of Christ as a liberating work, and, considering the fundamental importance of the concept of freedom throughout his argument in Galatians and its significance in his other letters as well, one might quite plausibly interpret his whole christology as a christology of liberation. According to one exegete at any rate, not only is it clear from Paul's "programmatic formulation" in Galatians 5:1 that "the apostle understands Christ, above all, as the great eschatological liberator," but one may also say that "Pauline theology in its deepest meaning is 'theology of freedom'" (Mussner: 14).

To this extent, the possibility of a christology of liberation is already confirmed by the New Testament, and it was with good reason that Martin Luther, for one, took his understanding of Christ in terms of freedom to be entirely appropriate, given the clear christological teaching of Paul and John. But could the same be said for us today?

According to the argument I developed in the preceding chapter, it is no longer sufficient to appeal simply to scripture or to the New Testament to establish the appropriateness of our christological formulations. Because we now know that even in the case of the Pauline letters, which are the earliest writings in the New Testament, what we have is already a formulation of still earlier Christian traditions, we also know that not even Paul can be judged an apostle in the strict sense of an original and originating witness to Jesus Christ. On the contrary, even Paul's witness and theology are already subject to the same question that we must put to our own— namely, whether, given the situation in and for which they were formulated, they are or are not appropriate to the normative witness of the apostles. Nor is this by any means a trivial question to which an affirmative answer is already obvious, as at once becomes apparent when one attends to two data that few New Testament scholars today would wish to question.

On the one hand, there is the fact that "in the Pauline sense, 'to be free' means to participate in Christ's crucifixion and resurrection" (Betz: 257). "I have been crucified with Christ," Paul says; "it is no longer I who live, but Christ who lives in me; and the life I now live in the flesh I live by faith

in the Son of God, who loved me and gave himself for me"
(Gal. 2:20). On the other hand, there is the fact that this
distinctively Pauline understanding of Christ's cross and resurrection as God's decisive act of liberation is completely
missing from the earliest stratum of Christian witness that we
are now in a position to reconstruct from our sources. As is
well known, there are but two places in the entire synoptic
tradition in which the cross is represented as the event of
salvation (Mark 10:45, 14:24), and both of these are exceptions
readily accounted for as originating relatively late in the
Hellenistic church. Otherwise there is no place in the earliest
tradition lying behind the synoptic gospels where Jesus'
death is understood to have the kind of saving significance
that Paul typically ascribes to it. On the face of it, then, Paul's
"theology of freedom," which in its very essence is "theology
of the cross," has all the appearance of a theological novelty,
whose appropriateness to the tradition of which it is presumably an interpretation is far from immediately obvious.

Of course, there is nothing in the least new about these
data. For almost a century now they have been widely recognized by historical-critical students of the New Testament,
and the issue of "Jesus and Paul" has been prominent on the
agenda of almost all revisionary christologies (Furnish, 1965).
But during most of this period, the usual way of dealing with
this issue has been to appeal to the so-called historical Jesus,
as distinct from the New Testament canon, as the real norm
for judging the appropriateness of Christian witness and theology. At an earlier stage, this appeal typically established
sufficient discontinuity between Jesus' own proclamation of
the reign of God and Paul's kerygma of the cross of Christ to
justify the call for a "return from Paul to Jesus." More recently, the same appeal has typically led to the conclusion
that, despite discontinuity in explicit christology, Paul's
kerygma can nevertheless claim sufficient support in Jesus'
own proclamation to be theologically justified. Because it

opens up, in effect, the same possibility of self-understanding before God that Jesus called persons to realize by his own summons to repentance and faith, it can be judged appropriate by reference to the real Christian norm in Jesus himself.

We have seen in earlier chapters that this typical procedure of more recent revisionary christology is open to fundamental objections, theological as well as historical. Given the nature of the sources available to us, it is simply impossible to establish as an empirical-historical conclusion that anything they contain in the way of a saying or deed of Jesus was in fact said or done by Jesus himself as distinct from being associated with him in the experience and memory of those to whom we owe the earliest traditions redacted in our sources (Bultmann, 1951a: 14–16). Consequently, if one assumes it to be necessary theologically to establish that a christology has support in what Jesus himself actually said and did before it can be judged to be appropriate, one places oneself in an impossible position. If a christology must indeed be shown to have such support in order to be judged appropriate, one is forced to admit that its appropriateness can never really be judged, because there can be no operational distinction in terms of empirical-historical evidence between Jesus as he actually was and Jesus as he was experienced and remembered by the earliest Christian witnesses. On the other hand, if one persists in maintaining that the appropriateness of a christology really can be judged after all, simply because it can be shown to have such support in the earliest stratum of Christian witness to Jesus, one is forced to abandon any assumption that it can be judged to be appropriate only because it can also be shown to have support in what Jesus himself actually said and did.

But if this dilemma reveals the historical objection to this typical assumption of revisionary christology, it is also open to the theological objection of implying that Jesus is other and less than even the earliest christology of witness asserts

or implies him to be. By making Jesus himself the primary
norm of appropriateness instead of the primal source of all
norms made fully explicit, one reduces him to but one authority among others, even if the primary such authority.
Thus he becomes the Jesus *with* whom we believe in God,
instead of the Jesus *through* whom we believe in God—one
who is a mere man, on the same level as ourselves, even if
first and foremost among us, instead of one who is infinitely
more than a mere man, on the same level with God, even if
also distinct from God as the decisive re-presentation of
God's gift and demand. As far as I am concerned, it is this
strictly theological implication that reveals the most serious
inadequacy in the typical procedure of revisionary christology. Even if the historical objection could somehow be
met by adducing primary as well as secondary sources about
Jesus, there would still be the decisive objection that the
Jesus attested by the Christian witness is infinitely other and
more than the so-called historical Jesus.

It would be wrong to infer from this, however, that there
is no positive theological significance in the quest of the historical Jesus, even in the form of the new quest of "post-
Bultmannian" theology (J. M. Robinson). Whatever the self-
understanding of those who have refined the methods and
produced the results of such a quest—and it is clear, I think,
that even the new questers have generally so understood
what they were doing as to be vulnerable to both of the
above objections—the fact remains that they have already
carried out just that work of historical reconstruction in
which we today must engage if we are to rightly locate the
real Christian canon. This is a fact, at any rate, if one accepts
the proposal I made in the preceding chapter and continues
to uphold the early church's own criterion of canonicity—
namely, that that alone is canonical which is also apostolic, in
the strict sense of being original and originating witness to
Jesus Christ. Precisely if one maintains this criterion of

canonicity, the first thing one must do in order to locate the canon satisfying this criterion is to reconstruct by critical analysis of the New Testament writings the history of tradition lying behind them. Only in this way can one establish the earliest and therefore apostolic stratum in this tradition. But this, of course, is exactly what one also has to do if one is to make any responsible empirical-historical judgments about Jesus himself, as distinct from even the earliest witness of the Christian community.

Consequently, even if one in no way shares the usual motives and objectives of the new quest of the historical Jesus, one may gratefully appropriate its methods and results as the very things that are needed by any christology of reflection in order to establish the appropriateness of its claims in our situation today. At the same time, by becoming clear that what one can and should seek by means of the quest is not the historical Jesus, but rather the earliest layer of Christian witness, one overcomes both of the objections to the procedure of most revisionary christologies. Whether Jesus did or did not say or do what he is represented as saying or doing in the earliest witness, one can still establish that this witness so represents him; and if one takes precisely this representation to be the apostolic and therefore canonical form of Christian witness, one takes it rather than Jesus to be the real norm of appropriateness, thereby allowing the Jesus to whom it bears witness to be no mere authority, but instead the explicit primal source of all authority, including its own.

Whether a christology of liberation is really possible, then, depends upon whether it can be shown to be appropriate to the witness of the apostles, and hence to the earliest stratum of Christian witness now available to us. This means that it must be shown to have support, not in Jesus himself, but rather in those very oldest traditions that any quest of the historical Jesus must perforce reconstruct, using our existing synoptic gospels as sources. Here, if anywhere, in these earliest Jesus-traditions, or, as Willi Marxsen prefers to say, in this earliest "Jesus-kerygma," we have what for us today must function as the real Christian canon or norm of appropriateness (Marxsen, 1968b: 108 f., 111; Ogden, 1976a; 1976b). Accordingly, the question we now have to ask is whether this norm does in fact support anything like the christology of liberation that the contemporary quest for freedom clearly seems to make necessary.

Obviously, any answer to this question requires that we first establish just what is to count as Jesus-kerygma and what is actually said or implied in it in the way of christological assertion. Considering the nature of these tasks and the difficulties of carrying them out, we will hardly be surprised that those who have undertaken them are by no means completely agreed about either the methods required or the results achieved by following the same methods. But if any answer to our question must to this extent be uncertain, we can undoubtedly be more confident of it than anyone can possibly be of any answer to the question of the historical Jesus. To judge from the assurances commonly given by theologians for whom a quest of the historical Jesus is theologically necessary, we can clearly have enough confidence in our answer to place it beyond reasonable doubt (Aulén: vii f., 99, 158; Küng, 1975: 137–157; Mackey: 12, 30, 50, 248, 256). Yet even if we discount these assurances as false, insofar as they are based on what is assumed to be theologically necessary rather than on what can be reasonably taken to be historically possible, there does, in fact, appear to be a certain consensus even among those who have pursued the quest of the historical Jesus in the most uncompromisingly critical way, whether in the earlier period represented by the monographs on Jesus of Rudolf Bultmann, Martin Dibelius, and Karl Ludwig Schmidt, or more recently, as represented by the similar works of Herbert Braun, Günther Bornkamm, and Hans Conzelmann (Bornkamm; Braun, 1969; Bultmann,

1951a; Conzelmann; Dibelius; Schmidt). Although even within this consensus, there are differences important enough to constitute what might be called "minimalist" and "maximalist" positions, and although many issues remain unsettled even among scholars occupying the same position, there nevertheless is considerable agreement both about what is to be counted as our earliest traditions and what is said or implied in these traditions concerning Jesus. My point is that this agreement can certainly give support to an answer to our question about the earliest stratum of Christian witness, whatever its bearing on the very different question about the historical Jesus. Therefore, I shall proceed to answer our question by attempting a brief summary of this scholarly consensus. If I orient myself in doing this to a "minimalist" rather than a "maximalist" type of position, my reason for doing so is simply to make the strongest possible case by depending solely on those features of the earliest Jesus-traditions about which scholars today are most fully in agreement.

According to the well-known summary in the Gospel of Mark, Jesus first appeared on the public scene as a prophet, proclaiming, "The time is fulfilled, and the reign of God is at hand; repent, and believe in the gospel" (1:15). Many scholars today would contend that these can hardly be the exact words in which Jesus would have formulated his proclamation. But even the most critical scholars are also generally agreed that Jesus did appear above all as an eschatological prophet, a proclaimer of the imminent reign of God, who conceived his own proclamation and the summons to repentance and faith that was of a piece with it to be the decisive word of God in the last hour. Thus, while he hardly called for faith in his own person, in the way in which he is represented as doing in the Gospel of John, he evidently did call for faith in his word, as itself the word of God that confronted his hearers with the definitive decision of their lives.

This is evident, indeed, even from sayings in which he most clearly looked forward to the coming of God's reign as still future and to the Son of Man as someone other than himself—or, in other words, from the very sayings that can be most certainly established as belonging to the earliest we have. So, for example, when he assured his hearers, "everyone who acknowledges me before men, the Son of Man also will acknowledge before the angels of God; but he who denies me before men will be denied before the angels of God" (Luke 12:8 f.; cf. Mark 8:38), he was not really pointing away from the present to the future, or away from himself to yet another. On the contrary, he was really making the most exalted claim for the decisiveness of the present moment and for the significance of himself and his words—asserting, in effect, that the final judgment of God was already taking place in his hearers' present response to his proclamation and that, insofar as they heard his word and did it, God's final salvation was even then open to them (Marxsen, 1960: 20–34).

The same understanding of himself as the bearer of God's word in the last hour also came to expression in the sayings in which he pointed to himself, or his words and deeds, as the "sign of the times." "Blessed are the eyes that see what you see! For I tell you that many prophets and kings desired to see what you see, and did not see it, and to hear what you hear, and did not hear it" (Luke 10:23 f.). If the queen of the South once came from the ends of the earth to hear the wisdom of Solomon, and if the men of Nineveh repented at the preaching of Jonah, "behold, something greater than Solomon is here. . . . something greater than Jonah is here" (Luke 11:31 f.). Or, again, he pointed to his exorcisms as signifying the breaking in of the reign of God and the end of Satan's power: "If it is by the finger of God that I cast out demons, then the reign of God has come upon you" (Luke 11:20). "No one can enter a strong man's house and plunder his goods, unless he first binds the strong man" (Mark 3:27).

Most explicitly of all, he saw in his own proclamation and healings a fulfillment of the prophetic promises of salvation (Isa. 35:5 f., 29:18 f., 61:1). "The blind receive their sight and the lame walk, lepers are cleansed and the deaf hear, and the dead are raised up, and the poor have good news preached to them. And blessed is he who takes no offense at me!" (Matt. 11:5 f.; cf. Luke 4:16–30).

A more complete summary than I can attempt here would also need to go into the fact that Jesus evidently appeared as a teacher or rabbi, not only as an eschatological prophet. By this I mean that his call to repentance and faith was not only made explicitly as an imperative summons, or implicitly by proclaiming the imminence of God's reign, but also—and again, implicitly—by definitively interpreting the will of God. Thus he explicated God's demand on his hearers in his continuing controversy with conventional legalism—as, for example, in the sayings familiar to us from the antitheses of the Sermon on the Mount, where he set the will of God sharply over against the traditional requirements of the law (Matt. 5:21–48), or in the many other sayings where he engaged in disputes concerning the sabbath and cultic purity and the great commandment. But aside from the fact that as teacher, also, Jesus implicitly laid claim to decisive significance, by representing his interpretation of God's will as definitive—"You have heard that it was said. . . . But I say to you. . . ."—his interpretation of God's will was in no way independent of his prophetic proclamation. Rather, it simply explicated the demand for repentance and faith implied by the overriding fact of the coming reign of God. In the final analysis, then, Jesus' role as teacher of the will of God, however important, stood in function of his primary role as the prophet of God's imminent reign.

But if the primacy of eschatology for Jesus can hardly be doubted, we still have to recognize that it was, after all, but the form of expression of his witness of faith, not the basic motif. Taken simply in itself, indeed, it is but the mythology of Jewish apocalypticism, whose terms and categories were well known and well used by many persons in Jesus' day whose answer to the existential question was significantly different from his own. It did serve, as we have seen, to express his implicit christological claim by representing his own proclamation and summons as the decisive act of the God whose reign was even then breaking in. Yet as important as it is to recognize Jesus' implied christology, it too remains purely formal if it is taken simply in itself. All that it can say is what it served to say to his hearers—namely, that the ultimate reality by which their existence was finally determined was none other than the God whose gift and demand were already confronting them through Jesus himself with the definitive decision for or against their own authentic existence.

But just who was this God whose gift and demand were already confronting them through Jesus? And what was the self-understanding that was thereby authorized as their authentic possibility?

These are clearly the critical questions in the new quest's interpretation of Jesus, and it is not surprising that, for all of their agreement on the essential point, different interpreters answer them in different ways. The answers that I myself take best to summarize their findings can be formulated as follows:

The God whose gift and demand were already made fully explicit in Jesus was the God of boundless love, from whom all things come and for whom they all exist; and the self-understanding that this God through Jesus both gave and demanded as one's authentic possibility was existence in faith in this boundless love—faith being understood in the twofold sense of trust in God's love alone for the ultimate meaning of one's life and, therefore, of loyalty to it and to all to whom it is loyal as the only final cause that one's life is to serve (Niebuhr, 1960: 16–23). In other words, the essential point, as I should put it, is that *Jesus meant love*—that the basic motif expressed both by his proclamation of God's reign and his summons to repentance and faith and by his implicit claim for their decisive significance was the motif of God's prevenient love as the gift and demand of authentic existence in faith and returning love.

Thus the reign of God whose coming he proclaimed was the reign of boundless love, by which even then the existence of his hearers was finally determined. Small wonder, then, that what he preached to the poor was good news: "Blessed are you poor, for yours is the reign of God. Blessed are you that hunger now, for you shall be satisfied. Blessed are you that weep now, for you shall laugh" (Luke 6:20 f.). But if the reign of God was nothing other than the reign of boundless love, freely offered to everyone who would receive it, the will of God was nothing other than the demand that one trustingly accept the gift of God's love and then loyally live in returning love for God and for all whom God loyally loves. "The first commandment is this, 'Hear, O Israel: The Lord our God, the Lord is one; and you shall love the Lord your God with all your heart, and with all your soul, and with all your mind, and with all your strength.' The second is this, 'You shall love your neighbor as yourself.' There is no other commandment greater than these" (Mark 12:29 ff.). Moreover, the love God demanded, like the love God gave, was boundless: "You have heard that it was said, 'You shall love your neighbor and hate your enemy.' But I say to you, love your enemies and pray for those who persecute you, so that you may be children of your Father who is in heaven; for he makes his sun rise on the evil and on the good, and sends rain on the just and on the unjust. . . . You, therefore, must be perfect, as your heavenly Father is perfect" (Matt. 5:43–48). By thus placing his hearers under the radical demand of God's love, Jesus made clear that they could not possibly be saved but by complete repentance. At the same time he summoned them to just such repentance, assuring them of the forgiveness of the God who has more joy over one sinner who repents than over ninety-nine righteous persons who need no repentance (Luke 15:7). In fact, he himself as the sign of God's loving reign was the bearer of God's forgiveness, the final proof of God's grace, in the last hour. This is why he could assure his hearers, "Blessed is he who takes no offense at me!"

According to those who have developed some such interpretation, it was this implicit claim of Jesus, to be the gift and demand of God's love made fully explicit, to which the early church responded with its explicit christological assertion. Even though Jesus hardly thought and spoke of himself as the Christ or the Son of Man, he evidently did point to himself and his word as being of decisive significance, in that already through him God was confronting his hearers with the gift and demand of boundless love and thus with the possibility of authentic existence in faith. Consequently, in thinking and speaking of Jesus as the Christ or as the Son of Man, the early church but affirmed explicitly, in such terms and categories as were available for the purpose, Jesus' own implicit claim to be the decisive revelation of God's love.

My own judgment is that something very like this account provides as reasonable an explanation as one can presently give of the origins of Christianity. By affirming that Jesus' own christology was at most implicit, it takes account of the fact that there is no explicit christology in the earliest stratum of Christian witness. On the other hand, by maintaining that Jesus' own proclamation and summons at least implied a christology, it explains the apostles' faith and witness as well as the early church's explicit christological assertion as the kind of responses to Jesus that they certainly appear to have been (Bultmann, 1967: 222 f., 451 f., 456–459). But in making the judgment that this is indeed a reasonable empirical-his-

torical account, I am quite certain that it is in no way necessary to a constructive christology of reflection such as I am
seeking to develop in this book. Whether Jesus did or did not
make the kind of claim of which the church's christological
assertion is the explication in no way alters the fact that, even
in the earliest stratum of witness accessible to us, what is
meant by Jesus—and the *only* thing that is meant by him—
is the one who makes or at any rate implies such a claim.
Provided, then, that this earliest witness is what for us must
count as the witness of the apostles, and hence as the norm
or canon for judging the appropriateness of all Christian witness and theology, the significant thing is not that Jesus at
least implicitly claimed to be the Christ, however probable
it may be that he did exactly that; rather, the significant thing
is that what the apostolic community understood by Jesus—
the Jesus to whom they themselves bore witness, implicitly
if not explicitly, as the Christ—was the one through whom
they had experienced, and who, through their own witness,
was still to be experienced as implying, just such a claim.

The sufficient evidence of this, it seems to me, is that even
this earliest witness of the apostles is precisely that—witness
of faith to Jesus, not historical report about him. Günther
Bornkamm introduces this distinction when he observes,
rightly, that "in narrating the history that once was [the
gospels] proclaim who Jesus is, not who he was" (Bornkamm:
15). Similarly, I am arguing, even if Jesus did in fact make or
imply the very christological claim he is represented as making or implying in the earliest stratum of witness—and, as I
have indicated, my own judgment is that one can reasonably
infer that he did—one still has to acknowledge that the point
of the witnesses in so representing him was not to report
what he did in the past, but rather to bear witness to what
he was doing in the present—not only to them, but through
their witness of faith also to their own hearers (Santayana:
4–19). Jesus, they claimed, is the one through whom both they

themselves and then, by means of their witness, all of their own hearers as well are decisively re-presented with the gift and demand of God's love, and hence with the possibility of authentic existence in faith and returning love. Accordingly, to accept their claim in no way requires one to assent to the truth of certain empirical-historical assertions about Jesus—to the effect that he himself made or implied the same claim now represented in their witness of faith. On the contrary, whatever the truth or falsity of any such empirical-historical assertions, to accept the claim represented in the apostolic witness as Jesus' claim is to accept a strictly existential-historical assertion—the assertion, namely, that *Jesus means love*—not that Jesus *meant* love, however true that may be also, but that Jesus *means* love, in the sense that through him the gift and demand of God's boundless love are made fully explicit as authorizing our own possibility of authentic faith and love.

But if Jesus who is said to be Christ means love in this sense, one may evidently say with Ernst Käsemann and others that Jesus also means freedom (Käsemann, 1968; Aulén: 162 f.; Hodgson: 208–264). Of course, neither Käsemann nor others who say this are content to say only this, but insist on the theological necessity of saying further that Jesus *meant* freedom. As a matter of fact, the claim is commonly made that Jesus not only meant freedom by proclaiming the liberating love of God and summoning his hearers to live in the freedom of God's children but himself also lived in such freedom, to the extent, indeed, of perfectly actualizing it in his own life. To claim anything less than this, it is held, would be to deprive the church's christological assertion about Jesus of a sufficient historical ground (Küng, 1975: 306 ff.; Van Buren: 109–134). But even if one argues, as I have argued earlier, that any such claim about Jesus' own perfect freedom is as theologically unnecessary as it is historically impossible, one can still join in affirming that the meaning of Jesus for us is precisely the possibility of the existence of freedom.

This is so at any rate insofar as one is willing to recognize that to exist in faith in God's boundless love for us and in returning love for God and for all whom God loves is to exist in radical freedom—both from and for oneself and all of one's fellow creatures. Because God's love for us is completely boundless and is offered to any and every person who is willing to receive it, nothing whatever can separate one from life's ultimate meaning. For this reason, to accept God's love through faith is to be freed from oneself and everything else as in any way a necessary condition of a meaningful life. But for the very same reason, the acceptance of God's love through faith establishes one's freedom *for* all things as well as one's freedom *from* them. Because God's love is utterly boundless and embraces everything within its scope, anything whatever is of ultimate significance and thus the proper object of one's returning love for God. In the case of other persons such as oneself, one can be thus free for them as the proper objects of one's love only by promoting their own freedom to be and to become fully themselves—active subjects of their own self-creation, instead of merely passive objects of the self-creations of others. In this sense, the existence of faith whose possibility is decisively re-presented through Jesus is a liberating as well as a liberated existence; it is an existence *for* the freedom of oneself and all others as well as an existence *in* the freedom that is the gift and demand of God's love (Ogden, 1979a: 41–65).

We may leave to the concluding chapter further discussion of the implications of such existence for freedom. The point I want to make here is simply that the earliest traditions concerning Jesus, which represent him as the gift and demand of God's love made fully explicit, evidently provide ample support for the christology of liberation that we are seeking. Provided that what one means by "liberation" is the existence of radical freedom established through faith in God's boundless love, there is no question that the chris-

tology even of the Jesus-kerygma is at least an implicit christology of liberation. The Jesus to whom it bears witness is the
one through whom the possibility of just such an existence of
radical freedom is decisively re-presented.

As for the further question of the appropriateness of Paul's
christology of freedom, which, as we saw, is in its very essence christology of the cross, it must suffice to say only this.
Despite the fact that the Jesus-kerygma makes no reference
whatever to the saving significance of the cross, it certainly
does represent Jesus, implicitly if not explicitly, as the decisive re-presentation of God, and thus as the one through
whom God has reconciled the world to himself. Therefore,
insofar as Paul's talk of the cross—or of the cross and the
resurrection—is simply his way of explicitly making this same
representation, in face of Jesus' crucifixion and in such terms
and categories as he had available to him in his situation, his
christology of the cross can claim sufficient support in the
witness of the apostles to be judged theologically appropriate. I should be willing to argue, although I cannot do so here,
that this is precisely how Paul's christology can best be interpreted (Marxsen, 1969: 160–170). By thinking and speaking of
the cross as the liberating judgment of God, Paul intends to
do nothing more than to make fully explicit the very claim
already made at least implicitly in the earliest stratum of
Christian witness—namely, that the Jesus who is said to be
Christ is the gift and demand of God's own love made fully
explicit. But if this is a correct interpretation, even Paul's
christology of liberation is far from being a theological novelty lacking all support in the apostolic witness. In fact, it is
an entirely appropriate formulation, given the possibilities
and limitations of his situation, of the witness of the apostles
to Jesus as the event of God's liberating love.

This is in no way to suggest, however, that it is in the terms
and categories of Paul's christology of the cross that we today
should seek to develop our own christology of liberation.

These terms and categories are no less mythological than those of the apocalyptic eschatology in which the earliest witness to Jesus was formulated, and we have no choice but to consistently demythologize the one as well as the other. Even so, the reason demythologizing is necessary is not only or even primarily because neither we nor our contemporaries any longer understand our existence in such mythological terms. Rather, the primary reason is that Paul's explicit christology of the cross is no more the basic motif of his witness of faith than the apocalyptic eschatology of the earliest Christian witnesses with its implicit christology was the basic motif of theirs. On the contrary, in the one case as surely as in the other, the mythology is but a form of expression, which, as such or taken simply in itself, has a purely formal meaning. For all of its importance, Paul's explicit christology of the cross, like the implicit christology of the apostles, could make no more than a purely formal claim—specifically, the claim that the ultimate reality finally determining all human existence is none other than the God who gave Christ up to die on the cross and, conversely, that "Christ crucified" is nothing less than the power and the wisdom of this God (Rom. 3:25, 8:32; 1 Cor. 1:23 f.). As exalted as this claim certainly is, the only thing that gives it its distinctive material meaning is *Jesus*—the Jesus about whom it is made and of whose decisive significance for human existence it is but one particular expression. In other words, the basic motif of Paul's christology, just as of any other christology that is really appropriate, is determined precisely and only by Jesus—the Jesus who means love and, therefore, also means freedom, because, being the gift and demand of God's love made fully explicit, he is the decisive re-presentation of our own possibility to be truly free.

It is this Jesus who is said to be Christ and who alone is the proper subject of any christology, whether of witness or of reflection. Because this is so, the christology of liberation that is demanded today by the pervasive concern for freedom is no less clearly supported by the apostolic witness. The Jesus who is there said to be Christ is the Jesus who sets us free— and, as Paul says, free precisely *for* freedom (Gal. 5:1).

7. God Who Gives Us the Victory through Our Lord Jesus Christ

Because the Jesus whom the earliest Christian witness asserts or implies to be Christ is the Jesus who means freedom, the christology of liberation that we are concerned to develop can evidently claim support in the normative witness of the apostles. This is so at any rate insofar as what one means by "liberation" is the freedom for which this Jesus sets us free: what Paul calls "the glorious freedom of the children of God," who so trust in the gift of God's boundless love that they are thereby free to live in loyalty to its demand (Rom. 8:21).

This argument implies, of course, that we may well include the predicate "liberator" among the terms and categories in which we seek to make the point of the christology of witness in our situation today. Provided liberation is understood to be just such an existence of trust in God's love and loyalty to it, Jesus as the one who decisively re-presents this existence as our authentic possibility can be asserted to be liberator, analogously to the way in which the early church asserted him to be Christ. To be sure, there is the important difference that the title "Christ," meaning "anointed one of God," expressly relates its bearer to God as one who acts on God's behalf, or in God's stead, whereas the title "liberator," meaning simply "one who sets us free," does nothing of the kind. Consequently, if "liberator" is to be properly asserted of Jesus as a christological predicate, it must be qualified as *"the*

Liberator," or "the liberator *of God*," understood as a subjective genitive that asserts Jesus to be the one through whom
God's own liberating love is made fully explicit as the gift and
demand of authentic faith. But in this respect "liberator" is
not essentially different from other terms that have been
used as christological predicates ever since the New Tes-
tament—such as, for instance, "savior" ($\sigma\omega\tau\dot{\eta}\rho$) or "lord"
($\varkappa\acute{\upsilon}\rho\iota o\varsigma$), both of which also had and have continued to
have secular as well as religious uses. The important point in
any event is that "liberator" can be an entirely appropriate
christological predicate insofar as it serves to make explicit
the claim clearly implied in the earliest Christian witness, if
not indeed in the witness of Jesus himself—namely, that Jesus
is the one through whom the liberating love of God that is the
ultimate reality determining our lives is decisively re-presented as making possible our own existence in freedom.

Our concern in this and the concluding chapter is with the
necessary implications of the formulation, "Jesus is the Liberator," in the sense of the one who sets us free for the freedom
of the children of God. Assuming, as I trust we may, that the
argument of Chapter 6 has sufficiently responded to the
question of the appropriateness of such a formulation, we are
still faced with the question of its credibility. But in order to
answer for its credibility, and hence to carry out our commitment to deal with the truth of the christology of witness as
well as with its meaning, we have to make explicit what this
formulation necessarily implies in the way both of metaphysical beliefs and of moral beliefs and actions. The reason
for this was already explained in Chapter 2 and may be
briefly summarized as follows.

We have seen that the christological assertion, in whatever
formulation, is by way of making explicit the claim already
at least implied in the earliest stratum of Christian witness.
I put the point in this way because it is difficult to determine,
given the sources on which we have to depend, to what

extent the christology of the earliest community was itself more than merely implicit. Certainly, in the very earliest Jesus-traditions that we considered in the last chapter, explicit christology seems entirely absent; and it is striking that even in the synoptic gospels themselves there are only two places (Matt. 18:6, 27:42) where anything is said about believing in Jesus himself, in the sense in which such faith is called for by the "Christ-kerygma" that is typical of the Gospel of John and most of the other New Testament writings (Marxsen, 1975: 36 f.). On the other hand, the form of kerygma that we find in the synoptic gospels clearly does involve the use of titles and other expressions of explicit christology, and so is not pure "Jesus-kerygma," but rather what Marxsen distinguishes as the third or mixed form of "Jesus Christ-kerygma" (Marxsen, 1968b: 111). Moreover, it is a reasonable inference that the Easter experience of the apostles very soon came to be expressed not only in the *"that"* of their witness, as Marxsen argues it originally was, but also in its *"what,"* to the extent that they explicitly confessed that by the resurrection God had made the prophet and teacher Jesus of Nazareth Messiah or Son of Man and that as such he would soon come (Marxsen, 1968b: 99; Bultmann, 1965: 45–56).

In any case, all formulations that either make or imply the christological assertion are formulations concerning Jesus that function to express his decisive significance for human existence. This they do by asserting or implying, in some terms or other, that he is the decisive re-presentation of ultimate reality, and hence the explicit primal source authorizing the authentic understanding of one's existence in relation to this ultimate reality. Thus, whether christological formulations consist in ascribing honorific titles to Jesus or in making exalted claims concerning his origin and destiny, the assertion they either make or imply is the existential-historical assertion that the understanding of existence explicitly authorized through him is one's authentic possibility of self-understanding in relation to ultimate reality.

But if this assertion thus answers the question of who or what Jesus is, this is certainly not the only question it answers. Precisely in asserting that Jesus is the decisive re-presentation of ultimate reality and hence the explicit primal source of authentic self-understanding, it also answers another question having two integrally related aspects—namely, who or what is the ultimate reality determining one's existence and who or what is one given and called to be by this same ultimate reality. This question it also answers because it asserts specifically that the ultimate reality determining one's existence is the boundless love of God and that, therefore, one is given and called to exist in faith in this love—in trust in its being freely given and in loyalty to what it demands. It thereby implies, however, not only the properly metaphysical assertion that ultimate reality is boundless love but also the properly moral assertion that one is so to act as to love all those who are embraced by this boundless love, taking all of their needs into account in determining one's concrete moral responsibility. This explains, then, why the question of the credibility of the christological formulation "Jesus is the Liberator" is the question of the credibility of these other assertions, metaphysical and moral, that it necessarily implies. If it is credible, they too must be credible; and unless they can be believed on the basis of our common human experience and reason, it cannot be believed on this basis, either.

Obviously, there are limits to what we can hope to do in these concluding chapters to answer this question of credibility. In fact, just as the argument in the preceding chapter did not so much establish the appropriateness of a christology of liberation as clarify conditions sufficient for establishing it, so the argument to which we now turn can do little more than to make clear conditions sufficient for establishing the credi-

mean by a categorial metaphysics. Suffice it to say here that it lies in the very nature of ultimate reality that it can be thought and spoken about in the terms and categories of our ordinary experience only by making use of these terms and categories in extraordinary ways. If they are to express what is really ultimate, their meaning must be generalized, and hence extended well beyond the limits within which we are accustomed to use them. The result is that they acquire new, relatively secondary senses as compared with the primary senses they ordinarily have.

Of course, there is nothing unusual about words acquiring such secondary senses. It happens all the time, as is clear from our regularly distinguishing between the "literal" meanings of words and what we call their "symbolic" or "metaphorical" meanings. But the important question so far as metaphysics is concerned is whether this distinction between the literal and the metaphorical meanings of words is exhaustive, or whether there is yet a third kind of meaning that certain words may have that cannot be simply identified with either of these other kinds.

The answer to this question that has been widely upheld by theologians in the main tradition of Christian theology is that there is indeed such a third kind of meaning, which they have distinguished from both the literal and the metaphorical kinds as properly "analogical." Thus, according to Thomas Aquinas, a properly analogical use of certain terms may be distinguished from any merely symbolic or metaphorical use because they designate perfections of which God, rather than any creature, is the primary exemplification. So, for example, the term "love" designates a perfection that is primarily exemplified by God and only secondarily exemplified by creatures. Consequently, when we say "God is love," we are saying something other and more than when we speak of God with the Psalmist as our "rock" or "fortress." Whereas the Psalmist's statement is obviously metaphorical in that it uses the words "rock" and "fortress" in relatively secondary senses, the claim that God is love is so far from being merely metaphorical as to be in a way literal. This is so, Aquinas argues, because with respect to what is meant by the word "love"—in his phrase, the "thing signified" by it *(res significata)*—its use as applied to God is really its primary use. And this is so, he maintains, even though with respect to how the word means—what he calls its "mode of signifying" *(modus significandi)*—its use as applied to God is indeed secondary, insofar as its primary sense is the sense it has as applied to a human being (Thomas Aquinas: 56–59, 66–71).

Aquinas's attempt thus to distinguish a properly analogical meaning for certain assertions about God is entirely of a piece with his whole classical metaphysical outlook. But an essentially similar attempt is typically made even by revisionary theologians whose approach to theology remains explicitly, if hardly classically, metaphysical. This is particularly striking in the case of Charles Hartshorne, whose very different kind of neoclassical metaphysics and natural theology in no way keeps him from developing a theory of analogy that is the exact counterpart to Aquinas's.

Thus, according to Hartshorne, there are "three strata of meaning in religious discourse," insofar as we quite properly use three different kinds of terms to speak of God. Two of these kinds are obvious enough and pose no particular problems. On the one hand, there are "plainly literal terms like relative or absolute," which cannot be applied to God at all unless they can be applied in exactly the same sense in which they are applicable to anything else. On the other hand, there are "plainly symbolic terms like shepherd or ruler," which are obviously applied to God in a very different sense from that in which they are primarily used of a human being with respect to the performance of a certain social role or function. But distinct from both of these kinds of terms, Hartshorne argues, there are certain other, problematic terms whose application to God is neither literal nor symbolic but analogical. This is the case, he contends, because "there is a legitimate broadest possible meaning of psychical terms [*sc.* like 'knowledge,' 'will,' and 'love'] which is applicable to all individuals whatever, from atoms to deity." Hartshorne allows, to be sure, that "if psychical terms like 'knowledge,' 'will,' 'love' . . . denote, as they tend to do, states or functions very like the human, then they are essentially in a class with shepherd, although not nearly so narrowly specific." But his contention is that the term "love," for example, need not denote merely human love or something very like it, but it can quite properly be given an utterly general sense in which its application to God is not symbolic but analogical. As a matter of fact, when "love" is understood in this analogical sense, it is precisely its application to God that is in a way the primary and, in this sense, literal use of the word. For it is God's love for us from which all other love is derived, and it is God alone who can be said to love literally or without restriction, all other love being in some way restricted and hence expressible only with qualification (Hartshorne, 1962: 133–147; 1970: 154 f.).

Readers acquainted with my own previous work will have recognized that I myself have long followed this same metaphysical approach, even if in the neoclassical form represented by Hartshorne, instead of the classical form represented by Aquinas (Ogden, 1977). The reason for this, quite simply, is my deep conviction that it is indeed God who is the ultimate ground of the freedom that is ours through Christ, so that anything like a christology without God could only be a self-contradiction. Nevertheless, as deeply convinced as I still am that metaphysical theism is necessarily implied by any adequate christological formulation, I have become increasingly skeptical of all forms of categorial metaphysics, neoclassical as well as classical. By this I mean that I no longer share the confidence that it is possible to give the kind of completely general and fundamental account that meta-physics exists to give by generalizing the meanings of our ordinary terms and categories so that they become proper metaphysical analogies. Let me now try to explain what I mean by this.

In general, I understand metaphysics to be the form of critical reflection whose purpose it is to make the necessary conditions of the possibility of anything whatever, and hence the first principles of all our thought and speech, fully explicit and understandable. Because these necessary conditions or first principles are strictly ultimate, and hence radically more general and fundamental than any of the conditions or prin-ciples designated by our ordinary terms and categories, they can be made thus fully explicit and understandable in one or the other of two ways: either strictly literally, in concepts and symbols all of which apply to the different things to which they are applied in the same sense or do not apply to them at all; or else analogically as well as literally, in concepts and symbols at least some of which apply to the different things to which they are applied in different senses that are the relatively primary or the relatively secondary senses of the terms. Insofar as one proceeds in the first of these ways, one develops a strictly literal, or, as I also say, "transcendental," metaphysics, whereas proceeding in the second way involves one in developing a partly analogical, or what I call "categorial," metaphysics.

Clearly, on this understanding of terms, Hartshorne's metaphysics, as much as Aquinas's, is a categorial metaphys-ics; and this is so even though the terms and categories Harts-horne chooses to generalize, or at any rate the meanings he takes them to have, are certainly very different from those of Aquinas's classical metaphysics. This explains why even a neoclassical metaphysics now seems to me to be open to serious question. For what I have more and more come to realize is that the whole notion of metaphysical analogy, on which any categorial metaphysics necessarily depends, involves serious logical difficulties.

This is not the place to go into these difficulties, much less to do justice to the ways in which categorial metaphysicians continue to try to overcome them. But such an extended discussion is hardly necessary anyhow, since the nub of the difficulties is fairly obvious and easy to understand. This can be brought out by recalling the distinction whereby classical metaphysicians, as we have seen, have tried to establish the possibility of a proper metaphysical analogy. I refer to Aquinas's distinction between what is meant by a word (the *res significata*) and how the word means (its *modus significandi*). Whereas in the case of a mere metaphor or symbol, there is no basis for this distinction, since the word is obviously used in a secondary sense, in the case of a proper analogy, the analogical sense of the word is its primary sense with respect to what is meant by it, even though its analogical sense is definitely secondary with respect to how it means. But now, as clear as this distinction may be in principle, there remains the obvious question of actually applying it; and it is here that one runs into serious difficulties as soon as one attempts to apply it metaphysically or to the unique case of God.

Unless God is already known, prior to the application of any word, there is no way of establishing that a word like "love" can be applied to God as a proper analogy as distinct from being merely a symbol. But this implies, then, that God must somehow be known immediately; for apart from an immediate knowledge of God, prior to the application of all words, one could not possibly know whether what is primarily meant by "love" is something about God, or rather merely something about human beings or other creatures. But, as is well known, the whole idea of "immediate knowledge," whether of God or of anything else, is radically problematic, insofar as "knowledge," by the very meaning of the word, is evidently mediate, in that it involves the use of concepts and symbols as well as our immediate experience. Consequently, although one may, and even must, speak of "an immediate *experience* of God"—universal experienceability being a necessary property of God as ultimate reality—one cannot speak coherently of "an immediate *knowledge* of God." This means that one simply cannot satisfy the condition necessary for distinguishing between a properly analogical and a merely metaphorical sense of the claim that God is love. Hence, for all one can ever possibly show to the contrary, this claim is in essentially the same class as such plainly symbolic claims as that God is shepherd or ruler.

Of course, there is the difference noted by Hartshorne that loving is not nearly so narrowly specific as being a shepherd. Moreover, there is the related difference that, whereas terms like "shepherd" or "ruler" are based in our external sense perception of ourselves and the natural and social world around us, the term "love" also has a basis in our internal nonsensuous perception of our own existence in relation to other persons. Consequently, one may well contend that the claim that God is love is, in any case, a more profound metaphor or symbol than the claim that God is our shepherd or ruler; and this contention can be further supported by arguing that such obviously symbolic claims as that God is our rock or fortress are doubly symbolic, in that the words "rock" and "fortress" are symbolic, in the first instance, of just such modes of personal being and relationship as are primarily denoted by a term like "love." But as true and as important as all this undoubtedly is, it in no way qualifies the essential point that, for all anyone is able to show to the contrary, even the profoundest metaphors or symbols about God are still only that, as distinct from being analogies in the proper sense of the word.

Nor do I find any reason to qualify this point in Hartshorne's occasional appeals to his panpsychist, or psychicalist, ontology. For, as much as I agree with him that this kind of a categorial ontology both implies and is implied by any consistent metaphysical theism that is likewise categorial, I encounter exactly the same difficulty in establishing the first as in establishing the second. In the nature of the case, any categorial ontology presupposes the possibility of a proper metaphysical analogy; for unless at least some terms or categories can be given utterly general, and hence properly analogical senses, there simply cannot be the concepts and symbols required by this kind of an ontology. But, then, it clearly will not do to appeal to such an ontology to establish the possibility of a categorial metaphysical theism. For unless and until one has first established the possibility of metaphysical analogy, thus to appeal to an ontology that itself could not be possible but for just this possibility is to beg the question.

Consequently, the conclusion to which I have finally come is that one can continue to make christology dependent on a categorial metaphysical theism only at the risk of its theoretical credibility. As a matter of fact, considering the seriousness of the difficulties that metaphysical analogy involves, I strongly suspect that this kind of a metaphysical theism can hardly be less of a problem in answering for the truth of christology than the mythological theism that I, at least, once intended to demythologize by it.

But to voice this suspicion is obviously to reopen the question whether the claim that the ultimate reality called "God" is boundless love ought not to be interpreted after all simply as a claim about ourselves, about our own freedom and responsibility to love our fellow human beings beyond any fixed limits. I find it significant in this connection that the contemporary philosopher of religion who, in my reading, has most acutely exposed the difficulties of metaphysical analogy has himself been led to embrace just such an understanding of theistic claims as in no way metaphysical or even cognitive (Palmer).

Even so, I am not yet willing to concede that this kind of theological reductionism, as I am compelled to regard it, is the only clear alternative to the categorial metaphysical theism I can no longer regard as credible. Quite the contrary, I am convinced that a strictly literal, and hence transcendental, metaphysical theism can still be reasonably defended; and I see no reason why such a theism, provided it is rightly developed, should not be entirely sufficient to establish the credibility of the strictly metaphysical implications of the christological assertion. In any event, there seem to me to be the best of reasons to continue to explore the possibility of such a third alternative, not only because the other two alternatives are both so patently inadequate, but also because there are clear indications in the work of those who have gone before us that such an alternative is indeed possible.

Without trying to take account of all such indications, I want to mention the work of the other thinker who, together with Hartshorne, has probably made the greatest impact on constructive philosophical theology in the contemporary English-speaking context. I refer to the work of Paul Tillich, which, like that of some of the other great theologians of his generation, currently tends to be neglected. Coming out of the tradition of German classical philosophy as well as the mystical religious tradition lying behind it, Tillich arrived in the United States having already developed in several major writings an exceedingly sophisticated philosophy of religion, or, as he later came to call it, "philosophical theology." Central to this theology was the claim that all our thought and speech about God is properly directed to "the Unconditioned," and therefore is and must be symbolic rather than literal. By his own account, however, he soon encountered an objection from the philosopher Wilbur Marshall Urban that led him finally to abandon or at least to qualify this claim. This was the objection, in effect, that, if all our thought and speech about God is symbolic, there can be no good reason to believe that any of it is cognitively significant. In other words, unless at least something literal can be thought and said about God, there is no way of excluding the possibility that all our allegedly symbolic thought and speech about God is either simply a misuse of concepts and symbols or else has some other, wholly noncognitive kind of meaning (Kegley and Brettall [eds.]: 333 f.).

Rightly feeling the force of this objection to his "pansymbolism," Tillich revised his original claim to allow that at least one literal statement can and must be made about God—namely, that God is being-itself. Actually, since this statement admits of a number of immediate inferences—such as, for example, that God is not *a* being, or that God transcends nonbeing absolutely—there are a number of statements about God that Tillich evidently made as being literally, rather than symbolically, true. Even so, one can find places in his later writings where he seems so reluctant to admit this as all but to revert to his original position, although, considering the seriousness of the objection that led him to abandon it, one is probably justified in concluding that he could hardly have ever really intended to return to it (Tillich, 1957: 9 f.).

Be this as it may, the really serious problem with Tillich's position, in my opinion, does not lie in any inconsistency in maintaining that certain literal statements can and must be made about God. Rather, the far more serious problem is that the only such statements that he himself was ever prepared to make were wholly one-sided. By this I mean that, as revisionary in many ways as Tillich's philosophical theology certainly was, its most basic premises remained, from first to last, those of a classical rather than of a neoclassical type of theism. Thus, while he could literally think and say that God is being-itself, he could not literally think and say that God is also *a* being—even though it is arguable that, since what is properly meant by "God" is the universal individual, it is precisely both of these claims together that constitute any adequate metaphysical theism: God is both, and literally both, being-itself *and* a being. Or, again, Tillich could say literally that God as being-itself, or "the absolute," transcends nonbeing absolutely; but when it came to speaking of God's relativity, or participation in nonbeing—what he himself meant by God as "creative life"—he was clear that the only statements one could make were not literal but symbolic (Tillich, 1951: 238 f., 270).

In short, Tillich's doctrine of God was unimpeachably classical in its one-sided preference for being over becoming, the absolute over the relative, the unchanging over the changing, the necessary over the contingent, and so on. In the case of each of these polar contrasts, he held that only the first of the two poles could be literally predicated of God, the second being thus predicable only symbolically. To be sure, he objected to the implication of the phrase "only a symbol," that symbolic predications are not really but only apparently true. But, so far as I can see, this implication has as much point in the case of his theology as in that of any classical theist. If the God who is not literally but symbolically relative is at the same time literally absolute, this God is also literally nonrelative, and so not really, but only apparently, relative after all.

Yet as seriously inadequate as Tillich's classical one-sidedness undoubtedly is, the possibility his work clearly seems to hold open is a metaphysical theism that would dispense altogether with proper analogy and, therefore, make a clean break with categorial metaphysics. In other words, in its essential formal structure, Tillich's mature analysis of religious discourse allows for only *two,* rather than three, strata of meaning, or kinds of terms.

On the one hand, there are the plainly literal terms whose meanings in religious discourse are exactly the same as their meanings in any other; they function primarily indicatively to denote the structure of reality in itself, and hence to identify what is properly named "God" and to distinguish it from everything else. On the other hand, there are the plainly symbolic terms whose meanings in religious discourse are different from the meanings they have in the other fields of discourse from which they are borrowed; they function primarily imperatively, to express the meaning of reality for us, and hence to call for the kind of self-understanding and moral action that are authorized by the ultimate reality called "God." In Tillich's own case, of course, the only terms that could be literally applied to ultimate reality involved a one-sided stress on being, and thus on the absolute, the unchanging, the necessary, and so forth. But this material difference in the only kind of metaphysics that Tillich himself was prepared to allow in no way invalidates the formal structure of his analysis or the claim it clearly implies—namely, that the only tenable metaphysics is strictly literal or transcendental and that such other nonliteral terms as we may and must use in speaking of God are one and all symbolic, not analogical.

My proposal is that we accept this formal claim and then explore the possibility of a materially different kind of transcendental metaphysics—specifically, a neoclassical kind, according to which God is literally becoming as well as being, and hence the relative as well as the absolute, the changing as well as the unchanging, the contingent as well as the necessary—in a word, the genuinely dipolar God whose transcendence of all things is, as Hartshorne says, precisely a "dual transcendence" (Hartshorne, 1970: 227–244). Although being transcendental instead of categorial, such a metaphysics would be formally different from Hartshorne's, even while being materially different from Tillich's, the extent of its formal difference ought not to be exaggerated. In the nature of the case, categorial metaphysics necessarily implies transcendental, and Hartshorne has, in fact, already laid the foundations for the strictly literal neoclassical theism that I am calling for. The import of my proposal, then, is that we should proceed to build on these foundations even as we follow Tillich's lead in cleanly breaking with all categorial metaphysics.

What I mean by this can be further clarified here only by returning to the implication with which we began, that God as ultimate reality is boundless love, and indicating briefly how I would now interpret it.

It will be evident from the preceding discussion that this implication as such can only be a symbolic rather than a literal metaphysical assertion. Because what we primarily mean by the word "love" is a certain way in which one human person exists and acts in relation to another, to speak of the love of God, where "God" is properly used to refer to strictly ultimate reality, is evidently to use the word in a secondary sense. This means among other things that the primary function of such speaking is not the properly metaphysical function of denoting the structure of ultimate reality in itself. Rather, its primary function is the properly religious (or possibly philosophical) function of so expressing the meaning of ultimate reality for us as to authorize the kind of existence and action on our part that are appropriate to it. Specifically, the claim that God as ultimate reality is boundless love means primarily that we ourselves are free to exist and act in love in relation to all our fellow creatures.

This, as I see it, is the important moment of truth in all noncognitivist theories of religious language generally and of theistic religious language in particular. Even though these theories may be mistaken—and, in my opinion, are mistaken —in concluding that the *only* function of such language is noncognitive, they are entirely justified in observing that it does function noncognitively, and that this is most especially so in the case of the symbolic stratum of such language. Whatever else the claim that God is boundless love may and even must be taken to mean, it must certainly be taken to mean that each of us is given and called to love beyond all of the limits of conventional human loving.

At the same time, even a symbolic metaphysical claim must imply certain assertions about the structure of ultimate reality in itself, else it could not be a true metaphysical claim at all. Moreover, unless it is to be "only a symbol" in the pejorative sense of being only apparently but not really true, the literal metaphysical assertions that alone suffice to make it true must assert all and not merely some of the conditions that are necessarily implied in making it. Thus, if to love another is above all to accept the other and then to act toward him or her on the basis of such acceptance, love necessarily implies not only acting on the other, but also, and just as surely, being acted on by the other—taking the other into account, letting him or her make a difference, and so on. Therefore, to assert truly, albeit symbolically, that God is boundless love necessarily implies not only that ultimate reality is individual as well as universal but also that this ultimate reality is acted on by all things just as surely as it acts on them. In other words, we must be able to assert not only truly but also literally that ultimate reality is a distinct center of universal *interaction* that, being acted on by all things as well as acting on them, is their sole final end as well as their only primal source.

Just this, of course, is what a neoclassical metaphysics allows—in fact, requires—one to assert. Given the premises of this kind of a transcendental metaphysics, it is just as literally true that the universal individual called "God" is *internally* related to all things, and hence acted on by them, as that this same individual is *externally* related to all things, and hence acts on them. Thus, unlike a classical metaphysics, which can literally assert only that God acts on everything but not that God is acted on by everything, a neoclassical metaphysics can literally assert *all* the conditions that are necessarily implied by the symbolic assertion that God is boundless love. Consequently, while its assertions, like those of any transcendental metaphysics, primarily function to denote the structure of ultimate reality in itself, they are in no way incoherent with the meaning of ultimate reality for us that is primarily expressed in speaking symbolically of the boundless love of God. On the contrary, by literally asserting all the necessary conditions of such speaking, they disclose it to involve a genuinely symbolic claim about the very structure of ultimate reality that is really and not only apparently true. They confirm that the same ultimate reality that is symbolically asserted to be the boundless love of God is literally the universal individual whose action on all others and reaction to all of their actions in turn are alike unsurpassable.

Is this to conclude, then, that a christology of liberation is really credible after all? Obviously, such a conclusion is not going to be accepted by anyone for whom all metaphysical claims, of whatever kind, exceed the bounds of credibility. Although I have indeed proposed that christology dissociate itself from all forms of categorial metaphysics, lest it be unable to answer for the truth of its claims, I have in no way countenanced the proposal of certain recent christologies that we should dispense with metaphysics altogether. Quite the contrary, I have left no doubt whatever that the christological formulation that Jesus is the Liberator necessarily implies the strictly metaphysical assertion that the ultimate ground of the freedom that Jesus decisively re-presents is the boundless love of God. Because it is precisely God who gives us the victory through our Lord Jesus Christ, and because any claim about God by its very nature implies a metaphysical claim, I have expressly insisted on the need for a transcendental metaphysics in order to confirm the truth of a christology of liberation. But if this is certain to raise questions about the credibility of such a christology for anyone who is skeptical of metaphysics, I fear I have not been able to do very much to answer these questions by arguing for the metaphysics on whose necessity I have insisted. To be sure, I have made clear that the foundations of such a metaphysics have already been laid by Hartshorne, and thus have appealed, in effect, to the weighty arguments that he has given to show that it is indeed credible when judged in terms of common human experience and reason. Even so, considering that I have been able to do no more than this, I would have no difficulty understanding if some of my readers would still have doubts about the credibility of my christological proposal.

At the same time, I think I have given reasons for holding that the christology of liberation I have proposed is in no way dependent on a categorial metaphysics. By frankly allowing that the assertion, "God is boundless love," although metaphysical, is a symbolic metaphysical assertion, I have set aside the serious difficulties of all attempts to establish its truth as properly analogical. In this way, my argument has faced up to what is perhaps the most formidable theoretical objection to any christology of reflection that takes full account of its metaphysical implications.

Still and all, the question of the theoretical credibility of its claims is not the only or even the most pressing question that a christology of liberation today has to answer. There remains the further question about the justice of its claims, and it is with this even more urgent question of their practical credibility that we will have to deal in the concluding chapter.

8. The Freedom We Have in Christ Jesus

At the outset of this discussion, I argued that no christology of reflection can be fully critical that does not concern itself with the truth of the christology of witness as well as with its meaning—or, as I also put it, that does not answer for the credibility of its claims as judged by common human experience and reason as well as for their appropriateness as judged by the normative witness of the apostles. Consequently, in the course of the discussion, in which I have tried to contribute toward such a christology of reflection, I concerned myself, first of all, with establishing the specific requirements of credibility and appropriateness in our situation today; second, with arguing for the appropriateness of a christology of liberation by showing that it can claim support in the apostolic witness to Jesus; and, third, with arguing for the credibility of such a christology to the extent of showing that its strictly metaphysical implications with respect to the structure of ultimate reality in itself can be made credible in terms of common human experience and reason, insofar as a neoclassical kind of transcendental metaphysics can be taken to formulate these terms. The task remaining for this concluding chapter is to continue the argument for the credibility of a christology of liberation by showing that its strictly moral implications as well may be said to be credible, given the specific requirements of credibility in the present situation.

We have seen that all christological formulations either assert or imply the constitutive christological assertion, according to which Jesus is of decisive significance for human existence because he is the decisive re-presentation of the meaning of ultimate reality for us, and thus explicitly authorizes our authentic self-understanding as human beings. This means that the christological assertion functions not only to answer the question of who Jesus is but also, and at one and the same time, to answer the question of who I am and of who or what the ultimate reality is by which my own existence and all existence are finally determined. As such, the christological assertion necessarily implies certain other assertions, both metaphysical and moral. Specifically, it implies both properly metaphysical assertions about the structure of ultimate reality in itself and properly moral assertions about human responsibility in relation to the others whose existence is always given together with our own. Because this is so, the question of the credibility of any christological formulation is the question of the credibility of these other assertions that it necessarily implies, moral as well as metaphysical. If it is credible, they too must be credible; and unless and until they can be shown to be credible in terms of our common experience and reflection simply as human beings, its credibility in such terms cannot be established.

Assuming that the preceding chapter at least clarified conditions sufficient to establish the credibility of the properly metaphysical implications of a christology of liberation, we must now consider its credibility in relation to its properly moral implications. Here too, however, I will be able to show that such a christology is credible only to the extent of clarifying conditions sufficient to establish its credibility.

I have argued that a christology of liberation is appropriate to the normative witness of the apostles and that, therefore, the formulation "Jesus is the Liberator" may very well be used in our situation today to make the constitutive christological assertion. In arguing so, however, I have also tried to make clear that I was thereby assuming a certain meaning for the term "liberation"—namely, what Paul refers to as

"the glorious freedom of the children of God" or, in yet
another phrase in his Letter to the Galatians, as "the freedom
we have in Christ Jesus" (Gal. 2:4). Just as any other christological formulation can be said to be appropriate only insofar
as the material meaning of its terms and categories is the
meaning determined precisely by Jesus, so Jesus can be appropriately thought and spoken of in terms of "liberation"
only insofar as it is understood to mean the freedom for
which precisely Jesus sets us free. It follows, then, that Jesus
may indeed be said to be the Liberator, but only provided
that "liberation" means the freedom we have in him, as
children of God who so trust in the gift of God's boundless
love for us and for all that we are thereby free both from and
for ourselves and everything else to live in loyalty to its demand.

But now is it not just this provision that renders the christology of liberation I have proposed really quite incredible?
Does it not make only too clear that the freedom we have in
Christ Jesus is something utterly general and abstract, and
thus completely different from the particular concrete freedoms, from want and oppression as well as from ignorance
and falsehood, with which men and women today are concerned? In fact, is it not perfectly obvious that talk about such
freedom really serves only to obscure the several struggles
for liberation by the oppressed against their oppressors, and
thus is so effectively ideological that it simply has to be
deideologized if it is ever to be credible?

These are the kinds of questions that certain theologians
have recently been pressing, and, in one way or another,
they have tried to deideologize talk of Christian freedom by
interpreting it politically in terms of Christian responsibility
to take sides in the various struggles for human liberation.
Thus they have interpreted the freedom we have in Christ
to mean the freedom of all the oppressed that we ourselves
are to help bring about by political action—by making use of

such power as is available to us to transform the basic structures of the existing social and cultural order so as to overcome the causes of oppression. The difficulty with such an interpretation, of course, is that political action for secular freedoms seems to be exactly that, and so itself hardly to be freedom, much less the freedom that is ours in Christ. And this difficulty becomes especially acute in the case of a "theology after the 'death of God,' " for which the only liberators there are are the merely human liberators who function as "representatives" of the God who is now known to be either dead or absent (Sölle, 1966; 1971: 71–89). But even in the case of other theologies where the being and activity of God are hardly in doubt, there is the clear tendency simply to identify the freedom we have in Christ with our own involvement in emancipatory struggles. Thus, so far from being, first of all, "the sacrament of the Father," Christ becomes simply "the way to the Father," and "going to God means making God real in history; it means building up God's kingdom here and now" (Sobrino: 350 f., 307; cf. xxiv).

There has naturally been a sharp reaction to such theologies as in effect, if not in intention, "the politicization of Christianity." According to Edward R. Norman, who has given expression to the reaction in these very terms, such politicization does not mean merely political activity on the part of Christians, but rather "the internal transformation of the faith itself, so that it comes to be defined in terms of political values—it becomes essentially concerned with social morality rather than with the ethereal qualities of immortality." Such transformation has come about, Norman argues, because, in their attempts to come to terms with the challenge of modern secularism, theologians and churches have lost sight of their own "rootedness in a spiritual tradition." "Instead of modifying or rejecting secular culture, the most influential of Christian thinkers have adopted it." More exactly, they have identified "Christian teachings" with "the

moral outlook and political ideals of liberalism," which is to
say, "democratic pluralism, equality, individualist human
rights, the freedom to choose values and so forth," all of
which are seen as "basic expressions of Christianity, the modern applications of the moral precepts of Christ." Consequently, "the emphasis of contemporary Christian interpretation of the Gospels is to see an activist, Humanist Christ,
whose message involved his followers in social transformation," even though "a reading of the Gospels less indebted to
present values . . . will reveal the true Christ of history in the
spiritual depiction of a man who directed others to turn away
from the preoccupations of human society" (Norman: 2, 11 f.,
7, 78).

As understandable as this reaction may be against certain
extreme forms of political interpretation of the christology of
witness, it too can assume a form that is clearly extreme. As
a matter of fact, Norman's interpretation of Christianity
seems to involve a separation of Christian faith and political
responsibility that is at least as objectionable as their identification. Thus, in protesting against contemporary Christianity's insistence on "the priority of social change over the
cultivation of personal spirituality," he goes so far as to say
that "morality is not the essence of Christianity—which is
about the evocation of the unearthly. Within Christianity,
morality is the structure of behaviour inherited by Jesus from
the Jewish tradition and confirmed by him; it is the discipline
which best enables men to order their lives that they might
discern the shadow of eternity cast over time; it is an educa-
tion of the soul. Moral behaviour—or love of neighbor, as
Christians call it—is an essential sign of the operation of faith.
But it is not itself Christianity, and in the Gospels the teachings of the Saviour clearly describes [sic] a personal rather
than a social morality" (79 f.).

If this representation of Christianity as involving a merely
"personal morality" directed toward educating the soul is

evidently the extreme contrary of its outright politicization, Norman does allow in at least one place that "in the world, the Christian seeks to apply the great love of God as well as he can in contemporary terms. And that will actually involve corporate social and political action." But it is significant, I think, that Norman no sooner makes this statement than he sharply qualifies it: "unlike the secular moralizers whom the Christian activists of the present day so closely resemble, the wise aspirant to eternity will recognize no hope of a better social order in his endeavours, for he knows that the expectations of men are incapable of satisfaction" (79).

Small wonder, then, that even a critic who is in general sympathetic with Norman's antidote to "the new Christian leftism" confesses to finding only a "negative" utility in his book. According to Peter L. Berger, Norman says so little that is positive about the sort of Christian political engagement he might approve of that a reader might well take him to suggest that "the only alternative to Marxist-oriented activism is an attitude of pessimistic detachment from all passionate involvement in the affairs of this world" (P. L. Berger: 53 f.).

A reader might well draw similar conclusions from any number of other recent criticisms of too simple an identification of Christian freedom and political responsibility. To give one more example, I may refer to Wolfhart Pannenberg's contribution to a controversy that broke out in Germany in the mid-1970s on the question, "Must Christians be socialists?" Arguing for a negative answer to this question, Pannenberg stresses the fundamental differences between "Jewish and Christian hope for the reign of God," and thus for "a reign of peace and justice in which all oppression of man by man is done away," and "the vision of a society of universal freedom and equality" that is at once the socialist and the liberal vision of the future. Whereas on socialist premises, the just society is to be brought about by doing away with private ownership of the means of production, the Christian expects its realization solely by the action of God. Consequently, not only is Christian hope connected with "a deep skepticism about all political revolutions that are brought about by human beings," but the Christian also knows that the peace and justice that are already possible even now are so, "in their full human meaning, only to the extent to which God comes to rule in human hearts." In this connection, Pannenberg stresses that "the real responsibility of the theologian" is to deal with the meaninglessness of modern society, in socialist countries no less than in capitalist ones, by addressing "the question of the meaning of human existence." In this way, "the rule of God in human hearts" can be shown to be "immediately relevant for whatever measure of justice and social peace may be possible in this world" (Teichert [ed.]: 63, 60, 65).

Here again, one can readily understand the concern to distinguish clearly between the reign of God that is the ultimate ground of Christian freedom and such transformation of society as may be the object of political responsibility. But surely the question Pannenberg also raises is whether he does not go so far as to separate the freedom we have in Christ from political responsibility for freedom and equality in human society. At any rate, this is the question that Helmut Gollwitzer forcefully presses in his concluding contribution to the controversy. Even if one rejects as unfounded Gollwitzer's claim that Pannenberg's Christian counterposition to socialism consists in "nothing else than late bourgeois skepticism and fear of change," it is hard to resist the gravamen of his charge that Pannenberg so understands what Karl Barth once called "the 'great' revolution of hope for the reign of God" that it rather becomes a "substitute" for "the 'small' revolutions of history" than providing the impulse and perspective for them. In fact, considering Pannenberg's pronounced pessimism about political action and his exclusive focus on the rule of God in human hearts, one can even understand Gollwitzer's parting shot when he observes that Karl Marx himself could hardly have written a more perfect confirmation of his criticism of religion (106).

It is by no means an idle question, then, whether the christology of liberation I have proposed is, in the final analysis, ideological. If the only alternative to simply identifying Christian freedom and political responsibility is simply separating them, the assertion of Christian freedom as well as the christological formulation presupposed by it is indeed ideological. By not so much as implying Christian responsibility to side with the oppressed in their struggles for secular freedoms, it functions in effect to stabilize the existing social and cultural order, providing at least a negative sanction for the structural injustices of this order.

Yet as convinced as I am of the soundness of this reasoning and of its direct relevance to the present christological discussion, I am far from convinced that the two alternatives that typically polarize this discussion are the only alternatives really open to us. On the contrary, I am persuaded by what seem to me good reasons that they are related to one another as extreme contraries, to which there is a third alternative, contradictory to each of them, and thus strong at both of the two points where they are respectively weak.

One reason I am persuaded of this is that it is quite possible —as the English language itself makes clear—to distinguish things without separating them and, therefore, to avoid separating things without identifying them. As a matter of fact, I should contend that the ability to do precisely this—to distinguish things, and hence neither to identify *nor* to separate them—is of the very essence of analytical thinking, whether in theology or anywhere else—just as, conversely, either to confuse things that are really distinct or to disjoin things that are really connected is to default as a critical thinker. But if this contention is sound, it must be possible at least in principle to avoid both of the usual alternatives in discussing Christian freedom and political responsibility, by neither simply identifying them nor simply separating them, but rather clearly distinguishing them—as really distinct and yet also really connected.

Furthermore, the achievements of those who have gone before us have already confirmed that just such a third alternative is a possibility in fact as well as in principle. One of the tragedies of much contemporary theology is that it has so exaggerated the novelty of the tasks that confront it—as well as, one suspects, the extent of its own abilities to accomplish them—that it has failed to benefit from work already done to carry out essentially the same tasks. The result is that, having ignored the lessons of the past, it has at best failed to accomplish its tasks as adequately as it might have and at worst fallen into the very errors that the past had already succeeded in avoiding. There is perhaps no place in recent theology where this result is more striking than in discussions of the question of Christian faith and political responsibility. As compared with treatments of this question by several theologians during the first half of this century, current treatments of it tend to appear insufficiently critical and lacking in balance, if not downright simplistic and one-sided.

This is particularly true, in my opinion, if one takes as a standard of comparison the lifelong work of Reinhold Niebuhr in dealing with this question. Niebuhr was as clear as any political theologian or theologian of liberation today that Christians simply as such have a political responsibility for "the good order and justice of our civil community." At the same time, he was also clear, as political theologians and theologians of liberation hardly are, that "Christians always live in a deeper dimension than the realm in which the political struggle takes place." On the other hand, unlike so many contemporary critics of political theologies and theologies of liberation, Niebuhr never allowed either his "Christian 'otherworldliness' " or his "Christian realism" to become an excuse for simply fleeing "the world of political contention into a realm of mystic eternity or moralistic illusion." Quite the contrary, he convincingly demonstrated that "such 'otherworldliness' is not an escape from history," but rather "gives us a fulcrum from which we can operate in history. It gives us a faith by which we can seek to fulfill our historic tasks without illusions and without despair." Similarly, his realism about the persistence of sin and self-interest at every level of human life was made to preserve rather than to destroy "a sense of responsibility for achieving the highest measure of order, freedom and justice despite the hazards of man's collective life" (Davis and Good [eds.]: 193, 196, 208, 195).

I am not suggesting by these comments either that Niebuhr's treatment of the question is beyond criticism or that there are not factors in our situation that do indeed make for tasks that are in part different from his. My point is simply that, even when one takes full account both of Niebuhr's limitations and of what really is new in our situation today, his achievement is still such as to remove any doubt that the polarization in current discussion can indeed be overcome (McCann).

Accordingly, I shall now attempt to do precisely this by arguing for a third alternative distinct from both of the usual answers to the question. I shall seek to show that, although the freedom we have in Christ Jesus is indeed different—I venture to say, infinitely different—from any and all secular freedoms, nevertheless the two kinds of freedom are also inseparable insofar as the moral implications of Christian freedom include the specifically political responsibility for the achievement of secular freedom.

The argument begins with the point that the freedom we have in Christ Jesus is the freedom whose ultimate ground is the liberating love of God and whose own essential nature is "faith working through love." Of course, this formulation also is Paul's. But we have already seen that his formulation may claim support in the apostolic witness to Jesus as the one through whom we are so re-presented with the gift and demand of God's love as to be explicitly confronted with the possibility of faith—the faith that is at once trust in the gift of God's love and loyalty to its demand. To be loyal to God's demand is to be loyal to God and to all the others to whom God is also loyal; and to understand this is to speak with Paul of love. In this sense, the freedom for which Christ has set us free is the freedom of love, both of God and, in God, of all whom God also loves.

But this means that our returning love for God and for all our fellow creatures in God is in its own way boundless, even as is the prevenient love of God for all of us. This is true, in one respect, in that the love demanded from us, like the love given to us, covers the full range of creaturely need. Because God's love knows no bounds and excludes nothing from its embrace, there is no creature's good that is not also God's good and no creaturely need that is not also a divine need. Consequently, in the case of fellow human beings like ourselves, whose needs are various and whose good is complex, even the least of their needs deserves to be met, and no part of their good is unworthy of realization. But the love demanded from us is boundless in another respect, in that it also governs the full scope of human responsibility. This is made clear by the first commandment that we shall love the Lord our God with all our heart, and with all our soul, and with all our mind, and with all our strength. Because nothing of ourselves is to be withheld from our love for God, all of our powers and all of the uses of our powers are regulated by this single commandment. Nor is this in any way qualified by the fact that there is also the second commandment that we are to love our neighbor as ourselves. On the contrary, because God's own love boundlessly includes all our neighbors as well as ourselves, the second commandment but makes explicit what is implicitly contained in the first. As a matter of fact, it is precisely by withholding nothing of ourselves from our love for our neighbors as well as for all of our fellow creatures that we can alone obey the first commandment. Therefore, it is just such love for God by loving all others in God that claims all that we are able to do and thus governs the whole extent of our moral responsibility.

The properly moral implications of Christian freedom, then, are the implications of a love for others that is boundless in this double respect, covering the full range of creaturely needs and regulating the full scope of human responsibility. Just what this love implies for moral action toward human beings is, of course, a variable insofar as it depends on some understanding both of the range of human needs and of the extent of human powers for meeting them. Because any such understanding obviously varies from one historical or cultural situation to another, any specification of the implications of love of neighbor is likewise subject to change. But what never changes is that love of neighbor always has just such properly moral implications and that they always pertain to doing all that lies within one's power toward meeting every genuine human need. For this reason, we may say that the properly moral implications of Christian freedom are always to seek justice, in the broad sense of so acting toward all others as to secure what is due them—to meet any and all of their real human needs and thus to realize the whole of their human good.

But if the love through which faith works in turn seeks justice and finds expression in it, is this not to say that Christian freedom does indeed imply political responsibility? So it may appear, and an argument to this effect is typical of political theologies and theologies of liberation. Jon Sobrino, for example, justifies the responsibility of present-day Christians to fashion and organize history by arguing that the Jesus

whom they are to follow "does not advocate a love that is
depoliticized, dehistoricized, and destructuralized. He advo-
cates a political love, a love that is situated in history and that
has visible repercussions for human beings." Sobrino recog-
nizes, to be sure, that "following" Jesus cannot be a matter
merely of "imitating" him, because of differences between
his situation and our own. But the only such difference that
Sobrino specifically mentions is that "Jesus himself expected
the imminent arrival of the kingdom." This expectation, he
allows, "could have a real impact and influence on the way
Jesus might envision the reorganization of society in terms of
justice and love, and . . . his view might differ radically from
that of people who see a long history ahead of them which
is to be fashioned and organized" (Sobrino: 369 f., 307, 389;
McDonald [ed.]: 105–122).

Even as thus qualified, however, Sobrino's argument will
hardly do. Quite aside from the obvious historical difficulties
of establishing Christian responsibility today by appeal to the
example of the historical Jesus, there is the evident anachronism involved in speaking of the love that Jesus advocated as
"a political love." Provided one means by the word "political" anything like what we today ordinarily take it to mean
—namely, the use of power to maintain or transform the
basic structures of society and culture—the love that Jesus
advocated could hardly have been a political love. Nor is the
reason for this, as Sobrino's qualifications might appear to
suggest, simply that Jesus looked forward to the imminent
coming of the reign of God and thus did not foresee a long
future during which history would need to be fashioned and
organized in terms of love and justice. The reason rather is
that the whole idea of human beings' having the power and
the responsibility to fashion and organize history is a very
recent idea that could no more have occurred to Jesus than
to any other person living in the ancient world.

Of course, there is nothing recent about the fact that

human beings are the kind of creatures who are given and called to create themselves and one another by creating their own history. So far as we are aware, to be human at all has always been to exist by somehow transforming the natural conditions of human life by establishing the distinctive order that we call society and culture. In this sense, it has always been true that human beings are uniquely historical beings who have the power and the responsibility to establish the social and cultural structures that shape their lives. But what has not always been true is that human beings are explicitly conscious of their unique historicity, and thus of the full scope of their power and responsibility to create themselves and one another. Quite the contrary, the clear consciousness that society and culture in all their forms are human creations is itself just such a creation, and a very recent one at that. It has emerged only gradually in connection with the revolutions, scientific and technological as well as social and political, that have created the modern secular world; and even now it is a force to be reckoned with only where secular society and culture have established themselves or somehow made an impact.

If this is so, however, it is plainly anachronistic to attribute to Jesus an understanding of human responsibility that necessarily presupposes such an explicit historical consciousness. On the other hand, the only way to avoid this anachronism is to frankly admit the insufficiency of any appeal simply to Jesus, or, for that matter, even to the witness of the apostles, in order to establish that the freedom that is ours in Christ implies a specifically political responsibility.

But as necessary as it is to make a frank appeal also to our distinctively modern historical consciousness, there can be no question about either the possibility of making this appeal or the conclusion to be drawn once it has been made. Without a doubt, those of us who are the beneficiaries of modern secularity are fully conscious that the whole of human society and culture is historical, in the strict sense of having at some time emerged and being even now maintained by the decisions of human beings such as ourselves. So far from being either supernaturally appointed or naturally given, all social and cultural forms are historically created—by men and women who are given and called to create themselves and one another by creating their own societies and cultures. To be sure, our power to create even the most basic social and cultural structures is a power that belongs to us as a species rather than as individuals. As individual persons, we are all far more the creatures of our societies and cultures than we are their creators. Furthermore, in every society known to us, there is a fundamental inequality between the few whose role in maintaining or transforming it is relatively active and the many whose role is correspondingly passive, in that they are more the objects of the self-creations of the few than the subjects of their own. In fact, if really to be a member of a society is to participate in the decisions by which its basic structures are maintained or transformed, most of the members of all existing societies are really nonmembers, insofar as they are cut off from any such participation.

But if it belongs to our historical consciousness thus to recognize the basic inequality between some individuals and others in our own, just as in every other, society, this recognition in no way qualifies our sense of the power that is ours as human beings. On the contrary, it compels the confession that the large majority of persons who, in one way or another, are more the victims of our society's decisions than their agents are insofar not yet free to be fully human beings.

But the whole effect of such historical consciousness, including this confession, is to extend the scope of our moral responsibility to include maintaining and transforming the very structures of society and culture. This must be so at any rate insofar as our moral responsibility is that implied by Christian freedom, and hence by the faith that works

through love. For, as we have seen, this love is doubly bound-less in that it covers the full range of creaturely need and governs the full scope of human responsibility. To become conscious, then, that even the basic structures of society and culture are subject to human power and that a fundamental need of every human creature is for a social and cultural order in which he or she is free to exercise such power is to realize at once that our moral responsibility as Christians has to include a specifically political responsibility. Because we know that we are each responsible for the whole social and cultural order of which we are a part, we also know that the love which seeks justice can no longer be only or even pri-marily a matter of meeting the needs that arise within the existing order. On the contrary, the primary, though not the only, task of such love is the specifically political task of trans-forming this very order—of so changing its basic structures that they more nearly meet the needs and secure the good of all of its members, and thus more nearly achieve the free-dom and equality that alone justify maintaining them.

The conclusion to which the argument leads, then, is that the freedom we have in Christ Jesus implies our specifically political responsibility for the achievement of secular free-dom. Actually, the implication here is twofold. For if Chris-tian freedom means that there should be justice, and hence freedom and equality, throughout society and culture, it also means that the majority who are more the victims than the agents of society's decisions have the *right* to demand such freedom and equality, even as the minority who are more the agents than the victims of the same decisions have the *re-sponsibility* to help the majority to achieve this right. Thus, although the two kinds of freedom are different and never to be identified, they are also conjoined and never to be sepa-rated—not at least by modern Christians like ourselves, now that we have become conscious of our proper human role as agents of history who bear full responsibility for the whole

social and cultural order. In fact, to share in this historical consciousness is to realize that the freedom for which Christ has set us free is so far from being something merely general and abstract as to involve us directly in all the struggles for particular concrete freedoms from want and oppression by all who suffer the injustices of existing society and culture.

But if this is the conclusion to be drawn from the argument, there is a certain corollary to it that we are also entitled to draw. I argued earlier that the only way to meet the specific requirements of credibility in the present situation is to devise methods for showing that the christology of witness is practically as well as theoretically credible. In this connection, I proposed the two methods that I called "deideologizing" and "political interpretation," and attempted to explain how they could meet these requirements. The question I did not further pursue, then, however, is whether these methods that clearly seem to be necessary, given the present theological situation, are also possible, in the sense of being appropriate when judged by the normative witness of the apostles. If the argument I have now presented is sound, the answer to this question can be immediately inferred to be affirmative. These theological methods are indeed appropriate, insofar as the apostolic witness to Jesus in no way intends to justify the interests of some human beings against the just interests of others, even though it clearly does have political implications, at least for us today, who have become aware of our specifically political power and responsibility.

Consequently, whenever we encounter a christological formulation whose function is ideological, we need have no hesitation in deideologizing it. Thus, for example, when we find Paul giving the Corinthians to understand that "the head of every man is Christ, the head of a woman is her husband, and the head of Christ is God," we have every reason to deideologize his sexist understanding of the relation between husband and wife—just as much reason, in-

deed, as Bultmann argues we have to demythologize the superstitious notion that Paul expresses later in the same chapter when he claims that an unworthy reception of the Lord's Supper results in physical illness and death (1 Cor. 11:3, 29 f.). In the one case quite as much as in the other, the claims expressed or implied are in no way supported by the apostolic witness to Jesus, but are simply expressions of the outlook of an age now past that by contemporary standards are either false or unjust.

On the other hand, deideologizing is something more than merely eliminating such unjust claims. In its positive meaning, indeed, it is the political interpretation whose appropriateness follows from the fact that the christological assertion necessarily has political implications for anyone possessed of historical consciousness and the corresponding sense of specifically political responsibility. Here too, of course, there is a parallel with the theological methods proposed by Bultmann—in this case with what he calls "existentialist interpretation." Just as one adequately interprets the christology of witness only when one makes clear the self-understanding that it authorizes, so one adequately develops this very self-understanding only when one spells out *all* its moral implications—not only for living within the existing social and cultural order but also for maintaining and transforming the basic structures of this order itself. Because the freedom that is ours in Christ clearly has specifically political implications, anything less than just such a political interpretation cannot possibly do justice to the christological assertion in any of its formulations.

Is a christology of liberation really credible after all, then? Certainly, for anyone for whom the limits of credibility do not exceed the strictly moral or political, the truth of the christology I have proposed must remain a problem. Unlike certain other christologies currently on the scene, it allows no one to suppose that the meaning of the christology of witness could ever be reduced to strictly moral or political terms. On the contrary, it expressly agrees with Luther that it is not enough nor is it Christian to appeal to the historical Jesus merely as the supreme example, whether of faith in God or of moral or political action. Aside from the evident historical difficulties of justifying such an appeal, there is the purely theological difficulty to which Luther draws attention when he insists, in terms borrowed from Augustine, that Christ is, first of all, a "sacrament" *(sacramentum)*, only secondly an "example" *(exemplum)* (Luther: 1:309; 2:141; 9:442; 10/1.1:10 ff.; 39/1:356; Lienhard: 21, 31, 64 ff., 79 f., 189). In other words, before Christ can be rightly taken as the true model for our own liberating love, he must first be taken as the real presence of the liberating love of God. It is for just this reason, indeed, that I have insisted, with all the classic expressions of the christology of witness in scripture and tradition, that the freedom we have in Christ can never be simply identified with secular freedom or with our political responsibility for achieving it.

On the other hand, I have also insisted that the two kinds of freedom are as inseparable as they are distinct, in that our political responsibility for achieving secular freedom follows necessarily from the freedom that is ours in Christ. Thus I have made clear that consistently deideologizing the christology of witness is as fully justified as consistently demythologizing it and that its political interpretation provides a necessary development of its existentialist interpretation. To this extent, the christology I have proposed would indeed seem to be credible practically as well as theoretically. So far from in any way sanctioning the want and oppression of the existing order, the assertion that Jesus is the Liberator is by strict implication the demand to do justice—above all, the kind of structural justice that can only be done politically, by continually transforming the basic structures of society and culture so as more nearly to achieve the equal freedom of all persons to be and to become themselves.

But this can hardly be the last word for any of us who are Christians and are therefore given and called to make this christological assertion. The clear implication of everything I have said is that we can make this assertion credibly only insofar as we ourselves, as individuals and as the community called church, also live up to the demand that it strictly implies—by involving ourselves in the ongoing struggles for basic justice, in solidarity with all who suffer from the oppressions of the existing order or are working to overcome them. To do anything less than this is to leave room for the question whether the freedom we have in Christ Jesus is not ideological, after all, whatever the conclusion of our christology of reflection.

Moreover, as this is the only way in which our christology of witness today can be credible, so it is also the only way in which our witness to Jesus Christ can be appropriate. For while our properly political responsibility as Christians is indeed distinctively modern, there is nothing in the least modern about the insistence that it is by what we do, not merely by what we think or say, that we are bound to bear this witness. On the contrary, one of the sayings attributed to Jesus in the earliest stratum of the synoptic tradition begins with the question, "Why do you call me 'Lord, Lord,' and not do what I tell you?" (Luke 6:46). And then, of course, there is the witness borne by the parable of the last judgment in Matthew 25:31-46. The utterly striking—in fact, mind-blowing—thing about this witness is that the criterion by which the nations are finally judged is in no way a christological, or even a theological, criterion. Not a word is said about believing in Christ, or even in God, but only about acting to meet the most ordinary of human needs. "I was hungry and you gave me food, I was thirsty and you gave me drink, I was a stranger and you welcomed me, I was naked and you clothed me, I was sick and you visited me, I was in prison and you came to me. . . . Truly, I say to you, as you did it to one of the least of these my brethren, you did it to me."

Without a doubt, we today can rightly hear this word only in terms of our specifically political responsibility. But thus to hear it and then to do it is exactly what is required if we are not only to talk about the point of christology but also to make it.

Works Consulted

ATTRIDGE, HAROLD W.
1979   " 'Heard Because of His Reverence' (Heb. 5:7)." *Journal of Biblical Literature*, 98: 90–93.

AULÉN, GUSTAF
1976   *Jesus in Contemporary Historical Research*, trans. Ingalill Hjelm. Philadelphia: Fortress Press.

BAILLIE, D. M.
1948   *God Was in Christ: An Essay on Incarnation and Atonement.* New York: Scribner.

BAILLIE, JOHN
1930   *The Place of Jesus Christ in Modern Christianity.* New York: Scribner.

BAUM, GREGORY
1979   *The Social Imperative.* New York: Paulist Press.

BENNETT, JOHN C.
1975   *The Radical Imperative: From Theology to Social Ethics.* Philadelphia: Westminster Press.

BERGER, KLAUS
1970–71 "Zum traditionsgeschichtlichen Hintergrund christologischer Hoheitstitel." *New Testament Studies*, 17: 391–425.

1973–74 "Die königlichen Messiastraditionen des Neuen Testaments." *New Testament Studies*, 20: 1–44.

BERGER, PETER L.
1979   "A Politicized Christ: Continuing the Discussion." *Christianity and Crisis*, 39: 52–54.

BETZ, HANS DIETER

1979   *Galatians: A Commentary on Paul's Letter to the Churches in Galatia.* Philadelphia: Fortress Press.

BOFF, LEONARDO, O.F.M.

1978   *Jesus Christ Liberator: A Critical Christology for Our Time,* trans. Patrick Hughes. Maryknoll, NY: Orbis Books.

BORNKAMM, GÜNTHER

1956   *Jesus von Nazareth.* Stuttgart: W. Kohlhammer Verlag.

BRAITHWAITE, R. B.

1955   *An Empiricist's View of the Nature of Religious Belief.* Cambridge: Cambridge University Press.

BRAUN, HERBERT

1962   *Gesammelte Studien zum Neuen Testament und seiner Umwelt.* Tübingen: J.C.B. Mohr.

1969   *Jesus, Der Mann aus Nazareth und seine Zeit.* 2d ed. Stuttgart: Kreuz Verlag.

BROWN, RAYMOND E., S.S.

1966   *The Gospel according to John.* Garden City, NY: Doubleday.

1968   *Jesus, God and Man.* London: Geoffrey Chapman.

1973   *The Virginal Conception and Bodily Resurrection of Jesus.* New York: Paulist Press.

1975   *Biblical Reflections on Crises Facing the Church.* New York: Paulist Press.

1977   *The Birth of the Messiah: A Commentary on the Infancy Narratives in Matthew and Luke.* Garden City, NY: Doubleday.

BULTMANN, RUDOLF

1951a   *Jesus.* Tübingen: J.C.B. Mohr.

1951b   "Neues Testament und Mythologie." In *Kerygma und Mythos,* Vol. 1, ed. H. W. Bartsch. 2d ed. Hamburg: Herbert Reich–Evangelischer Verlag: 15–48.

1952a   *Glauben und Verstehen,* Vol. 2. Tübingen: J.C.B. Mohr.

1952b   "Zum Problem der Entmythologisierung." In *Kerygma und Mythos,* Vol. 2, ed. H. W. Bartsch. Hamburg: Herbert Reich–Evangelischer Verlag: 179–211.

1953   *Das Evangelium des Johannes.* 13th ed. Göttingen: Vandenhoeck & Ruprecht.

1954   *Glauben und Verstehen,* Vol. 1. 2d ed. Tübingen: J.C.B. Mohr.

1964   *Die Geschichte der synoptischen Tradition.* 6th ed.
Göttingen: Vandenhoeck & Ruprecht.

1965   *Theologie des Neuen Testaments.* 5th ed. Tübingen:
J.C.B. Mohr.

1967   *Exegetica, Aufsätze zur Erforschung des Neuen Testaments,* ed. Erich Dinkler. Tübingen: J.C.B. Mohr.

CADBURY, HENRY J.

1937   *The Peril of Modernizing Jesus.* New York: Macmillan.

CALVERT, D.G.A.

1971–72 "An Examination of the Criteria for Distinguishing the
Authentic Words of Jesus." *New Testament Studies,* 18:
209–218.

CAMPENHAUSEN, H. F. VON

1968   *Die Entstehung der christlichen Bibel.* Tübingen:
J.C.B. Mohr.

CHRISTIAN, WILLIAM A.

1964   *Meaning and Truth in Religion.* Princeton, NJ: Princeton University Press.

COBB, JOHN B., JR.

1971   "A Whiteheadian Christology." In *Process Philosophy
and Christian Thought,* ed. Delwin Brown, Ralph E.
James, Jr., and Gene Reeves. Indianapolis, IN: Bobbs-
Merrill: 382–398.

1975   *Christ in a Pluralistic Age.* Philadelphia: Westminster
Press.

CONZELMANN, HANS

1959   "Jesus Christus." In *Religion in Geschichte und Gegenwart,* Vol. 3, ed. Kurt Galling. 3d ed. Tübingen: J.C.B.
Mohr: 619–653.

CONZELMANN, HANS and LINDEMANN, ANDREAS

1976   *Arbeitsbuch zum Neuen Testament.* 2d ed. Tübingen:
J.C.B. Mohr.

DAVIS, HARRY R. and GOOD, ROBERT C. (eds.)

1960   *Reinhold Niebuhr on Politics: His Political Philosophy
and Its Application to Our Age as Expressed in His
Writings.* New York: Scribner.

DIBELIUS, MARTIN

1939   *Jesus.* Berlin: Walter de Gruyter.

DODD, C. H.

1970   *The Founder of Christianity.* New York: Macmillan.

EBELING, GERHARD

1959   *Das Wesen des christlichen Glaubens.* Tübingen: J.C.B. Mohr.

FAUT, S.

1907   *Die Christologie seit Schleiermacher, Ihre Geschichte und ihre Begründung.* Tübingen: J.C.B. Mohr.

FLEW, ANTONY and MACINTYRE, ALASDAIR (eds.)

1955   *New Essays in Philosophical Theology.* London: SCM Press.

FORSYTH, P. T.

1909   *The Person and Place of Jesus Christ.* Boston: Pilgrim Press.

FREI, HANS W.

1975   *The Identity of Jesus Christ: The Hermeneutical Bases of Dogmatic Theology.* Philadelphia: Fortress Press.

FULLER, REGINALD H.

1965   *The Foundations of New Testament Christology.* New York: Scribner.

1966   *A Critical Introduction to the New Testament.* London: Duckworth.

1971   *The Formation of the Resurrection Narratives.* New York: Macmillan.

FURNISH, VICTOR PAUL

1965   "The Jesus-Paul Debate: From Baur to Bultmann." *Bulletin of the John Rylands Library,* 47: 342–381.

1979   *The Moral Teaching of Paul.* Nashville, TN: Abingdon.

GAGER, JOHN G.

1974   "The Gospels and Jesus: Some Doubts about Method." *Journal of Religion,* 54: 244–272.

GEERTZ, CLIFFORD

1973   *The Interpretation of Cultures: Selected Essays.* New York: Basic Books.

GERRISH, B.A.

1975   "Jesus, Myth, and History: Troeltsch's Stand in the 'Christ-Myth' Debate." *Journal of Religion,* 55: 13–35.

GOGARTEN, FRIEDRICH

1965   *Die Verkündigung Jesu Christi, Grundlagen und Aufgabe.* 2d ed. Tübingen: J.C.B. Mohr.

1966   *Jesus Christus Wende der Welt, Grundfragen zur Christologie.* Tübingen: J.C.B. Mohr.

GOULDER, MICHAEL (ed.)

1979   *Incarnation and Myth: The Debate Continued.* London: SCM Press.

GRASS, HANS

1956   *Ostergeschehen und Osterberichte.* Göttingen: Vandenhoeck & Ruprecht.

1973   *Christliche Glaubenslehre,* Vol. 1. Stuttgart: W. Kohlhammer Verlag.

GREEN, MICHAEL (ed.)

1977   *The Truth of God Incarnate.* London: Hodder & Stoughton.

GRIFFIN, DAVID R.

1973   *A Process Christology.* Philadelphia: Westminster Press.

GRILLMEIER, ALOYS, S.J.

1975   *Christ in Christian Tradition,* Vol. 1: *From the Apostolic Age to Chalcedon,* trans. John Bowden. 2d ed. Atlanta, GA: John Knox Press.

GUTIÉRREZ, GUSTAVO

1976   "Faith as Freedom: Solidarity with the Alienated and Confidence in the Future." In *Living with Change, Experience, Faith,* ed. Francis A. Eigo. Villanova, PA: Villanova University Press: 15–54.

HAHN, FERDINAND

1963   *Christologische Hoheitstitel, Ihre Geschichte im frühen Christentum.* Göttingen: Vandenhoeck & Ruprecht.

HAHN, FERDINAND, LOHFF, WENZEL, and BORNKAMM, GÜNTHER

1962   *Die Frage nach dem historischen Jesus.* Göttingen: Vandenhoeck & Ruprecht.

HARNACK, ADOLF VON

1950   *Das Wesen des Christentums.* Stuttgart: Ehrenfried Klotz Verlag.

HARTSHORNE, CHARLES

1962   *The Logic of Perfection and Other Essays in Neoclassical Metaphysics.* La Salle, IL: Open Court.

1970   *Creative Synthesis and Philosophic Method.* La Salle, IL: Open Court.

HARVEY, VAN A.

1966   *The Historian and the Believer: The Morality of Historical Knowledge and Christian Belief.* New York: Macmillan.

1976   "A Christology for Barabbases." *The Perkins School of Theology Journal,* 29, 3: 1–13.

HARVEY, VAN A. and OGDEN, SCHUBERT M.
1962   "Wie neu ist die 'Neue Frage nach dem historischen Jesus'?" *Zeitschrift für Theologie und Kirche,* 59: 46–87.

HEIDEGGER, MARTIN
1927   *Sein und Zeit.* Halle: Max Niemeyer.

HENGEL, MARTIN
1975   *Der Sohn Gottes, Die Entstehung der Christologie und die jüdisch-hellenistische Religionsgeschichte.* Tübingen: J.C.B. Mohr.

HERRMANN, WILHELM
1892   "Der geschichtliche Christus der Grund unseres Glaubens." *Zeitschrift für Theologie und Kirche,* 2: 232–273.

1908   *Der Verkehr des Christen mit Gott im Anschluss an Luther dargestellt.* 5th & 6th ed. Stuttgart: J. C. Cottasche Buchhandlung Nachfolger.

1913   *Die mit der Theologie verknüpfte Not der evangelischen Kirche und ihre Überwindung.* Tübingen: J.C.B. Mohr.

HICK, JOHN
1958   "The Christology of D. M. Baillie." *Scottish Journal of Theology,* 11: 1–12.

1966   "Christology at the Crossroads." In *Prospect for Theology: Essays in Honour of H. H. Farmer,* ed. F. G. Healy. London: James Nisbet: 137–166, 233–234.

HICK, JOHN (ed.)
1977   *The Myth of God Incarnate.* London: SCM Press.

HODGSON, PETER C.
1976   *New Birth of Freedom: A Theology of Bondage and Liberation.* Philadelphia: Fortress Press.

HOOKER, M. D.
1970–71 "Christology and Methodology." *New Testament Studies,* 17: 480–487.

HOULDEN, J. L.
1977   *Patterns of Faith: A Study in the Relationship between the New Testament and Christian Doctrine.* London: SCM Press.

KÄHLER, MARTIN
1956   Der sogenannte historische Jesus und der geschicht-
        liche, biblische Christus, ed. Ernst Wolf. 2d ed. Münch-
        en: Christian Kaiser Verlag.
KÄSEMANN, ERNST
1954   "Das Problem des historischen Jesus." Zeitschrift für
        Theologie und Kirche, 51: 125–153.
1968   Der Ruf der Freiheit. 4th ed. Tübingen: J.C.B. Mohr.
1975   "Die neue Jesus-Frage." In Jésus aux origines de la
        christologie, ed. Jean Dupont. Gembloux: J. Duculot:
        47–57.
KÄSEMANN, ERNST (ed.)
1970   Das Neue Testament als Kanon, Dokumentation und
        kritische Analyse zur gegenwärtigen Diskussion. Göt-
        tingen: Vandenhoeck & Ruprecht.
KASPER, WALTER
1974   Jesus der Christus. Mainz: Matthias Grünewald Verlag.
KECK, LEANDER E.
1971   A Future for the Historical Jesus. New York: Abingdon
        Press.
KEGLEY, CHARLES W. and BRETTALL, ROBERT W. (eds.)
1952   The Theology of Paul Tillich. New York: Macmillan.
KELLY, J.N.D.
1950   Early Christian Creeds. London: Longmans, Green.
KERTELGE, KARL (ed.)
1974   Rückfrage nach Jesus, Zur Methodik und Bedeutung
        der Frage nach dem historischen Jesus. Freiburg:
        Herder Verlag.
KIERKEGAARD, SØREN
1936   Philosophical Fragments, Or a Fragment of Philoso-
        phy, trans. David F. Swenson. Princeton, NJ: Princeton
        University Press.
KNOX, JOHN
1952   Criticism and Faith. Nashville, TN: Abingdon-Cokes-
        bury Press.
1955   The Early Church and the Coming Great Church.
        Nashville, TN: Abingdon Press.
1957–58 "The Church Is Christ's Body." Religion in Life, 27:
        54–62.
1958   Jesus: Lord and Christ. New York: Harper & Brothers.

1962   *The Church and the Reality of Christ.* New York: Harper & Row.

KÜNG, HANS

1975   *Christ sein.* 6th ed. München: R. Piper Verlag.

1980   "Toward a New Consensus in Catholic (and Ecumenical) Theology." *Journal of Ecumenical Theology,* 17: 1–17.

LEHMANN, MARTIN

1970   *Synoptische Quellenanalyse und die Frage nach dem historischen Jesus, Kriterien der Jesusforschung untersucht in Auseinandersetzung mit Emanuel Hirschs Frühgeschichte des Evangeliums.* Berlin: Walter de Gruyter.

LIENHARD, MARC

1980   *Martin Luthers christologisches Zeugnis, Entwicklung und Grundzüge seiner Christologie,* trans. Robert Wolff. Göttingen: Vandenhoeck & Ruprecht.

LOHSE, BERNHARD

1963   *Epochen der Dogmengeschichte,* Stuttgart: Kreuz Verlag.

LÜHRMANN, DIETER

1975   "Die Frage nach Kriterien für ursprüngliche Jesusworte—eine Problemskizze." In *Jésus aux origines de la christologie,* ed. Jean Dupont. Gembloux: J. Duculot: 59–72.

LUTHER, MARTIN

1883–   *D. Martin Luthers Werke, Kritische Gesamtausgabe.* Weimar: Hermann Böhlau.

MACHOVEC, MILAN

1972   *Jesus für Atheisten,* trans. Paul Kruntorad. Stuttgart: Kreuz Verlag.

MACKEY, JAMES P.

1979   *Jesus, the Man and the Myth: A Contemporary Christology.* New York: Paulist Press.

MACKINTOSH, H. R.

1913   *The Doctrine of the Person of Jesus Christ.* 2d ed. Edinburgh: T. & T. Clark.

MARSHALL, I. HOWARD

1976   *The Origins of New Testament Christology.* Downers Grove, IL: Inter-Varsity Press.

MARXSEN, WILLI

1960 *Anfangsprobleme der Christologie.* Gütersloh: Gütersloher Verlagshaus Gerd Mohn.

1964 *Die Auferstehung Jesu als historisches und als theologisches Problem.* Gütersloh: Gütersloher Verlagshaus Gerd Mohn.

1968a *Die Auferstehung Jesu von Nazareth.* Gütersloh: Gütersloher Verlagshaus Gerd Mohn.

1968b *Das Neue Testament als Buch der Kirche.* Gütersloh: Gütersloher Verlagshaus Gerd Mohn.

1969 *Der Exeget als Theologe, Vorträge zum Neuen Testament.* 2d ed. Gütersloh: Gütersloher Verlagshaus Gerd Mohn.

1975 *Die Sache Jesu geht weiter.* Gütersloh: Gütersloher Verlagshaus Gerd Mohn.

1976a "Christology in the New Testament." In *The Interpreter's Dictionary of the Bible: Supplementary Volume,* ed. Keith Crim. Nashville, TN: Abingdon: 146–156.

1976b "The New Testament: A Collection of Sermons." *The Modern Churchman,* 19: 134–143.

1978 *Einleitung in das Neue Testament, Eine Einführung in ihre Probleme.* 4th ed. Gütersloh: Gütersloher Verlagshaus Gerd Mohn.

McCANN, DENNIS P.

1981 *Christian Realism and Liberation Theology: Practical Theologies in Creative Conflict.* Maryknoll, NY: Orbis Books.

McDONALD, DURSTAN R. (ed.)

1979 *The Myth/Truth of God Incarnate.* Wilton, CT: Morehouse-Barlow.

McINTYRE, JOHN

1966 *The Shape of Christology.* London: SCM Press.

METZ, JOHANN BAPTIST

1977 *Glaube in Geschichte und Gesellschaft, Studien zu einer praktischen Fundamentaltheologie.* Mainz: Matthias Grünewald Verlag.

MONTEFIORE, H. W.

1962 "Towards a Christology for Today." In *Soundings: Essays Concerning Christian Understanding,* ed. A. R. Vidler. Cambridge: Cambridge University Press: 147–172.

MOULE, C.F.D.
1977   *The Origin of Christology.* Cambridge: Cambridge
          University Press.
MUSSNER, FRANZ
1976   *Theologie der Freiheit nach Paulus.* Freiburg: Herder
          Verlag.
NIEBUHR, H. RICHARD
1941   *The Meaning of Revelation.* New York: Macmillan.
1960   *Radical Monotheism and Western Culture.* New York:
          Harper & Brothers.
NINEHAM, DENNIS
1976   *The Use and Abuse of the Bible: A Study of the Bible
          in an Age of Rapid Cultural Change.* London: Macmil-
          lan Press.
1977   *Explorations in Theology 1.* London: SCM Press.
NORMAN, EDWARD R.
1979   *Christianity and the World Order.* Oxford: Oxford Uni-
          versity Press.
NORRIS, RICHARD A., JR. (ed.)
1980   *The Christological Controversy.* Philadelphia: Fortress
          Press.
NORTH, ROBERT (ed.)
1971   *In Search of the Human Jesus.* New York: Corpus In-
          strumentorum.
O'COLLINS, GERALD, S.J.
1977   *What Are They Saying About Jesus?* New York: Paulist
          Press.
OGDEN, SCHUBERT M.
1971   "The Task of Philosophical Theology." In *The Future of
          Philosophical Theology,* ed. Robert A. Evans. Philadel-
          phia: Westminster Press: 55–84.
1975a   "On Revelation." In *Our Common History as Chris-
          tians: Essays in Honor of Albert C. Outler,* ed. John
          Deschner, Leroy T. Howe and Klaus Penzel. New York:
          Oxford University Press: 261–292.
1975b   "The Point of Christology." *Journal of Religion,* 55:
          375–395.
1975c   "The Criterion of Metaphysical Truth and the Senses of
          'Metaphysics.'" *Process Studies,* 5: 47–48.
1976a   "The Authority of Scripture for Theology." *Interpreta-
          tion,* 30: 242–261.

1976b "Sources of Religious Authority in Liberal Protestant-ism." *Journal of the American Academy of Religion,* 44: 403–416.

1976c "Christology Reconsidered: John Cobb's 'Christ in a Pluralistic Age.'" *Process Studies,* 6: 116–122.

1977 *The Reality of God and Other Essays.* 2d ed. New York: Harper & Row.

1978 "Theology and Religious Studies: Their Difference and the Difference It Makes." *Journal of the American Academy of Religion,* 46: 3–17.

1979a *Faith and Freedom: Toward a Theology of Liberation.* Nashville, TN: Abingdon.

1979b *Christ without Myth: A Study Based on the Theology of Rudolf Bultmann.* 2d ed. Dallas, TX: Southern Methodist University Press.

1981 "The Concept of a Theology of Liberation: Must a Christian Theology Today Be So Conceived?" In *The Challenge of Liberation Theology,* ed. L. Dale Richesin and Brian J. Mahan. Maryknoll, NY: Orbis Books: 127–140.

PALMER, HUMPHREY

1973 *Analogy: A Study of Qualification and Argument in Theology.* London: Macmillan Press.

PANNENBERG, WOLFHART

1964 *Grundzüge der Christologie.* Gütersloh: Gütersloher Verlagshaus Gerd Mohn.

PELIKAN, JAROSLAV

1971 *The Christian Tradition,* Vol. 1: *The Emergence of the Catholic Tradition (100–600).* Chicago: University of Chicago Press.

PERRIN, NORMAN

1976 *Rediscovering the Teaching of Jesus.* 2d ed. New York: Harper & Row.

PEUKERT, HELMUT (ed.)

1969 *Diskussion zur "politischen Theologie."* Mainz: Matthias Grünewald Verlag.

PITTENGER, W. NORMAN

1959 *The Word Incarnate: A Study of the Doctrine of the Person of Christ.* New York: Harper & Brothers.

1970 *Christology Reconsidered.* London: SCM Press.

1974   "The Incarnation in Process Theology." *Review and Expositor*, 71: 43–57.

1977   "Christology in Process Theology." *Theology*, 80: 187–193.

RAHNER, KARL, S.J.

1962   *Schriften zur Theologie*, Vol. 1. 6th ed. Zürich: Benziger Verlag.

1972   *Schriften zur Theologie*, Vol. 10. Zürich: Benziger Verlag.

1975   *Schriften zur Theologie*, Vol. 12. Zürich: Benziger Verlag.

1976   *Grundkurs des Glaubens, Einführung in den Begriff des Christentums.* Freiburg: Herder Verlag.

RAHNER, KARL, S.J. (ed.)

1977   *Befreiende Theologie, Der Beitrag Lateinamerikas zur Theologie der Gegenwart.* Stuttgart: W. Kohlhammer Verlag.

RAHNER, KARL, S.J. and THÜSING, WILHELM, S.J.

1972   *Christologie—systematisch und exegetisch.* Freiburg: Herder Verlag.

RAHNER, KARL, S.J. and WEGER, KARL-HEINZ, S.J.

1979   *Was sollen wir noch glauben? Theologen stellen sich den Glaubensfragen einer neuen Generation.* Freiburg: Herder Verlag.

RISTOW, HELMUT and MATTHIAE, KARL (eds.)

1960   *Der historische Jesus und der kerygmatische Christus, Beiträge zum Christusverständnis in Forschung und Verkündigung.* Berlin: Evangelische Verlagsanstalt.

RITSCHL, ALBRECHT

1888   *Die christliche Lehre von der Rechtfertigung und Versöhnung*, Vol. 3: *Die positive Entwicklung der Lehre.* 3d ed. Bonn: Adolf Marcus.

ROBINSON, JAMES M.

1959   *A New Quest of the Historical Jesus.* London: SCM Press.

ROBINSON, J.A.T.

1973   *The Human Face of God.* London: SCM Press.

SANTAYANA, GEORGE

1946   *The Idea of Christ in the Gospels or God in Man.* New York: Scribner.

SCHÄFER, ROLF
1972   *Jesus und der Gottesglaube.* 2d ed. Tübingen: J.C.B. Mohr.

SCHEFFCZYK, LEO (ed.)
1975   *Grundfragen der Christologie heute.* Freiburg: Herder Verlag.

SCHIERSE, FRANZ JOSEF (ed.)
1972   *Jesus von Nazareth.* Mainz: Matthias Grünewald Verlag.

SCHILLEBEECKX, EDWARD, O.P.
1963   *Christ the Sacrament of the Encounter with God,* trans. Paul Barrett, Mark Schoof, and Laurence Bright. New York: Sheed & Ward.
1979   *Jesus: An Experiment in Christology,* trans. Hubert Hoskins. New York: Seabury Press.
1980   "I Believe in Jesus of Nazareth: The Christ, the Son of God, the Lord." *Journal of Ecumentical Studies,* 17: 18–32.
1981a   *Christ: The Experience of Jesus as Lord,* trans. John Bowden. New York: Crossroad.
1981b   *Interim Report on the Books Jesus and Christ,* trans. John Bowden. New York: Crossroad.

SCHLEIERMACHER, FRIEDRICH
1960   *Der christliche Glaube nach den Grundsätzen der Evangelischen Kirche im Zusammenhange dargestellt,* ed. Martin Redeker. 7th ed. Berlin: Walter de Gruyter.
1967   *Über die Religion, Reden an die Gebildeten unter ihren Verächtern,* ed. Rudolf Otto. 6th ed. Göttingen: Vandenhoeck & Ruprecht.

SCHLIER, HEINRICH
1935   "ἐλεύθερος χτλ." In *Theologisches Wörterbuch zum Neuen Testament,* Vol. 2, ed. Gerhard Kittel. Stuttgart: W. Kohlhammer Verlag: 484–500.

SCHMIDT, KARL LUDWIG
1929   "Jesus Christus." In *Religion in Geschichte und Gegenwart,* Vol. 3, ed. Hermann Gunkel and Leopold Zscharnack. 2d ed. Tübingen: J.C.B. Mohr: 110–151.

SCHMITHALS, WALTER
1972   *Jesus Christus in der Verkündigung der Kirche, Aktuelle Beiträge zum notwendigen Streit um Jesus.* Neukirchen-Vluyn: Neukirchener Verlag.

SCHOONENBERG, PIET, S.J.
1971   *The Christ: A Study of the God-Man Relationship in
          the Whole of Creation and in Jesus Christ,* trans. Della
          Couling. New York: Herder & Herder.

SCHULZ, SIEGFRIED
1972   "Die neue Frage nach dem historischen Jesus." In
          *Neues Testament und Geschichte, Oscar Cullmann
          zum 70. Geburtstag,* ed. Heinrich Baltensweiler and Bo
          Reicke. Zürich: Theologischer Verlag/Tübingen: J.C.B.
          Mohr: 33–42.
1975   "Der historische Jesus, Bilanz der Fragen und Lösung-
          en." In *Jesus Christus in Historie und Theologie, Neu-
          testamentliche Festschrift für Hans Conzelmann zum
          60. Geburtstag,* ed. Georg Strecker. Tübingen: J.C.B.
          Mohr: 3–25.

SCHWEITZER, ALBERT
1951   *Geschichte der Leben-Jesu-Forschung.* 6th ed. Tübin-
          gen: J.C.B. Mohr.

SOBRINO, JON, S.J.
1978   *Christology at the Crossroads: A Latin American Ap-
          proach,* trans. John Drury. Maryknoll, NY: Orbis
          Books.

SÖLLE, DOROTHEE
1966   *Stellvertretung, Ein Kapitel Theologie nach dem "Tode
          Gottes."* 3d ed. Stuttgart: Kreuz Verlag.
1971   *Politische Theologie, Auseinandersetzung mit Rudolf
          Bultmann.* Stuttgart: Kreuz Verlag.

STRECKER, GEORG
1969   "Die historische und theologische Problematik der
          Jesusfrage." *Evangelische Theologie,* 29: 453–476.

TEICHERT, WOLFGANG (ed.)
1976   *Müssen Christen Sozialisten sein? Zwischen Glaube
          und Politik.* Hamburg: Lutherisches Verlagshaus.

TE SELLE, EUGENE
1975   *Christ in Context: Divine Purpose and Human Possibil-
          ity.* Philadelphia: Fortress Press.

THOMAS AQUINAS
1964   *Summa Theologiae,* Vol. 3: *Knowing and Naming God*
          (Ia. 12–13), ed. Herbert McCabe, O.P. New York:
          McGraw-Hill.

TILLICH, PAUL
1951   *Systematic Theology*, Vol. 1. Chicago: University of Chicago Press.
1957   *Systematic Theology*, Vol. 2. Chicago: University of Chicago Press.
TRACY, DAVID
1975   *Blessed Rage for Order: The New Pluralism in Theology*, New York: Seabury Press.
TROELTSCH, ERNST
1911   *Die Bedeutung der Geschichtlichkeit Jesu für den Glauben.* Tübingen: J.C.B. Mohr.
VAN BUREN, PAUL M.
1963   *The Secular Meaning of the Gospel.* New York: Macmillan.
WHITEHEAD, ALFRED NORTH
1925   *Science and the Modern World.* New York: Macmillan.
1933   *Adventures of Ideas.* New York: Macmillan.
WILES, MAURICE
1967   *The Making of Christian Doctrine: A Study in the Principles of Early Doctrinal Development.* Cambridge: Cambridge University Press.
1974   *The Remaking of Christian Doctrine.* London: SCM Press.
1976   *Working Papers in Doctrine.* London: SCM Press.
1979   *Explorations in Theology 4.* London: SCM Press.
YERKES, JAMES
1978   *The Christology of Hegel.* Missoula, MT: Scholars Press.
ZAHN-HARNACK, AGNES VON
1951   *Adolf von Harnack.* 2d ed. Berlin: Walter de Gruyter.
ZAHRNT, HEINZ
1960   *Es begann mit Jesus von Nazareth, Die Frage nach dem historischen Jesus.* 4th ed. Stuttgart: Kreuz Verlag.
ZIOLKOWSKI, THEODORE
1972   *Fictional Transfigurations of Jesus.* Princeton, NJ: Princeton University Press.
1978   "Jesus between Theseus and Procrustes." *Bulletin of the Midwest Modern Language Association,* 11: 53–61.

Index

J

Jesus, Jesus Christ, *passim;* as the decisive re-presentation of God/ultimate reality, 58, 59, 76, 77, 78, 79, 81, 82, 83, 87, 112, 121 f., 124, 125, 129, 130, 131, 149; as eschatological prophet, 115, 117; as the explicit primal source of authentic self-understanding, 42, 78, 87 f., 129, 130; as first of all "sacrament," only secondly "example," 166; as a fully human being, 12, 72 f.; as the gift and demand of God's love made fully explicit, 76, 87, 120, 122, 123, 124, 125, 158; as he actually was, 16 f., 44, 53, 55, 67, 111; as he was experienced and remembered by the earliest Christian witnesses, 53, 55, 67, 111; as the Liberator, 127 f., 130, 131, 146, 149 f., 166 f.; as the primal *source* of authority, not *an* authority, 79, 81, 102, 113; as teacher, 117; being of, in himself, 16, 23, 29, 41, 59, 60, 62, 65, 84, 87; death of, 110; empirical-historical, 56 f., 58, 59 f., 64 f., 87; existential-historical, 56 f., 59 f., 64 f., 87; exorcisms of, 116 f.; faith of, 68–72, 73 ff.; formal/ material identity of, 16, 43, 56; implicit christological claim of, 118 f., 120, 121; meaning of, for us, 16, 23, 29, 41, 59, 60, 62, 65, 82, 85, 87, 122; means freedom, 122 f., 125, 127; means love, 122, 125; religion *of/about,* 45 f.; resurrection of, 77, 129; self-understanding of, 17 f., 58, 61, 65 f., 67 f., 69–72, 74 f., 77 ff., 87; sinlessness of, 74; so-called historical, 16 f., 43 f., 48, 49, 50, 51, 52, 53, 56, 87, 98, 101, 110, 112, 114, 160, 166; traditions about, 46 f., 49 f., 51, 53 f., 58 f., 101, 113 f., 115, 123, 129; work of, 108. *See also* Christological formulations; Christological predicates; Christological titles; Christology; God; Quest of

the historical Jesus; Ultimate reality
John, 51, 76, 108 f.; Gospel of, 115, 129. *See also* Fourth Gospel
Justice, 91, 93, 94, 95, 96, 106, 147, 159, 160, 163, 166 f.

K

Kähler, Martin, 46, 51
Käsemann, Ernst, 49, 50, 52, 53, 122
Kelly, J. N. D., 21
Kenoticism, 10
Kerygma, 47, 48 f., 51, 52, 53, 55, 73, 110, 129; Christ-, 51, 129; Jesus-, 51, 53 f., 58, 114, 124, 129; Jesus Christ-, 129
Kierkegaard, Søren, 71 f.
Knowledge, 137 f.
Knox, John, 77, 100, 103
Küng, Hans, 114, 122

L

Legend, 21, 74, 75, 79. *See also* Assertions, legendary
Letter to the Galatians, 108 f., 150
Liberal Protestantism, 97 f.
Liberation, 106 f., 123 f., 127 f., 149 f. *See also* Freedom
Lienhard, Marc, 166
Lincoln, Abraham, 56 f.
Lohse, Bernhard, 1
Love, 69, 72, 119, 122, 123, 130, 132, 133 f., 135, 137, 138, 144 f., 158 f., 160, 163, 166
Luke, Gospel of, 76
Luther, Martin, *xiii,* 109, 166

M

Mackey, J. P., 71 f., 114
Magisterium, 98
Mark, Gospel of, 46, 76, 115
Marshall, I. H., 77
Marx, Karl, 155
Marxsen, Willi, 24, 51–55, 57 ff., 114, 116, 124, 129
Matthew, Gospel of, 1, 23 f., 28, 76
McCann, D. P., 157
Meaning, 2 ff., 5, 22, 86, 88, 89, 128, 131, 132, 148, 165 f.
Meaning of Revelation, The, 56

Schleiermacher, Friedrich, 7, 12, 13, 33 f.
Schlier, Heinrich, 108
Schmidt, K. L., 47, 114 f.
Schmithals, Walter, 28
Schweitzer, Albert, 46
Science, 6, 89 f., 131, 161
Scripture, 5, 6, 20, 44 f., 48, 50, 97–100, 109; and tradition, 97 f., 99 f.; historical-critical study of, 99–102. *See also* Canon; Christology, New Testament; New Testament
Second Vatican Council, 13, 98
Secularism, 91, 151
Secularity, 92, 161
Self-understanding, 6, 11, 69 f., 78, 83, 118, 132, 143, 165; authentic, 17, 27, 30, 34 f., 37, 42, 59, 65, 69, 70, 72, 75, 76, 78, 82 f., 87, 118, 129 f., 149. *See also* Human existence
Sexism, 92, 164 f.
Sin, 157
Sobrino, Jon, 91, 151, 159 f.
Socialism, 153 f.
Society, social order, 90, 92, 95, 154, 155, 161 f., 164, 165; secular, 161; structures of, 95 f., 151, 160, 161, 162, 163, 165, 166 f.
Sölle, Dorothee, 151
Sola scriptura, 97 f., 104
Source criticism, 46, 99, 101
Symbol, 137, 138, 142, 145. *See also* Words, meanings of, symbolic
Synoptic gospels, 45, 46, 51, 53, 54, 55, 73, 74, 99, 101, 110, 113, 121, 128, 129. *See also* Luke, Gospel of; Mark, Gospel of; Matthew, Gospel of
Synoptic tradition, 47, 74, 99, 101, 110, 167; earliest stratum of, 47, 51, 58 f., 113, 167. *See also* Witness, earliest

T
Technology, 89 f., 161
Temptation stories, 74
Theism, 75, 78, 135, 139, 140, 141 f.; classical, 7, 141, 142; neoclassical, 141, 143. *See also* God; Metaphysics; Religion, theistic

Theological method, 93–96, 105, 164 f. *See also* Theology
Theology, *xi*, 2, 3 f., 11, 90, 97, 98, 101, 104, 110, 121, 133, 155; academic, 91; "after the 'death of God,' " 151; Anglican, 10; dialectical, 48; kerygmatic, 48; liberal, 48, 90, 104; liberation, 91 f., 156 f., 159; Lutheran, 10; natural, 132, 134; neo-orthodox, 90, 97; of the cross, 110; of the social gospel, 90; philosophical, 131, 132, 140, 141; political, 91, 156 f., 159; "post-Bultmannian," 55, 112; postliberal, 90; Protestant, 13, 97–100; revisionary, 5, 68, 90 f., 134; Roman Catholic, 13, 97–100. *See also* Christology; God; Reflection, theological; Theological method; Ultimate reality
Thomas Aquinas, 133–137
Thüsing, Wilhelm, 84
Tillich, Paul, 7, 140–144
Tradition criticism, 99, 101
Trent, Council of, 98
Truth, 2 ff., 5, 11, 22, 52, 77 f., 83, 84, 86, 88, 89, 91, 93, 96, 106, 128, 131, 132, 139, 146, 148, 165

U
Ultimate reality, *x*, 16, 26 f., 28, 29, 30, 32, 34, 35, 36, 41 f., 69, 78, 82 f., 94, 118, 125, 128, 129, 130, 131 f., 133, 139, 149; meaning of, for us, 34 f., 36, 37, 39, 42, 59, 82 f., 87, 143, 144 ff., 149; structure of, in itself, 34, 36, 82 f., 142 f., 144 ff., 148, 149. *See also* God; Jesus, Jesus Christ; Metaphysics
Urban, W. M., 140

V
Van Buren, P. M. 122, 132

W
Weger, K.-H., 66, 80
Whitehead, A. N., 23, 28 f.
Wiles, Maurice, 9
Witness, 2, 11, 14, 51, 52, 55, 56, 61, 62, 64 f., 74, 79, 83, 90, 92, 95,

124911